ABOLITION AND THE PRESS

Medill School of Journalism
VISIONS *of the* AMERICAN PRESS

GENERAL EDITOR
David Abrahamson

Selected titles in this series

ABOLITION
AND THE PRESS

THE MORAL STRUGGLE
AGAINST SLAVERY

Ford Risley

MEDILL SCHOOL OF JOURNALISM

Northwestern University Press

Evanston, Illinois

Northwestern University Press
www.nupress.northwestern.edu

Printed in the United States of America

10   9   8   7   6   5   4   3   2   1

Library of Congress Cataloging-in-Publication Data

Risley, Ford.
    Abolition and the press : the moral struggle against slavery / Ford
Risley.
       p. cm. — (Visions of the American press)
    Includes bibliographical references and index.
    ISBN 978-0-8101-2507-0 (pbk. : alk. paper)
    1. Slavery—Press coverage—United States—History—19th
century. 2. Antislavery movements—Press coverage—United States—
History—19th century. 3. Antislavery movements—United States—
Periodicals—History—19th century. 4. Antislavery movements—
United States—History—19th century. 5. Abolitionists—United
States—Biography. 6. Journalism—Political spects—United States—
History—19th century. 7. American newspapers—History—19th
century. I. Title. II. Series.
E449.R57 2008
071´.3—dc22
                                                                          2008027949

♾ The paper used in this publication meets the minimum requirements of the
American National Standard for Information Sciences—Permanence of Paper
for Printed Library Materials, ANSI Z39.48-1992.

To my mother and father

CONTENTS

PREFACE

◈

This book examines the role that nineteenth-century abolitionist newspapers played in working to end slavery in the United States. It is the story of a group of devoted men and women who for more than four decades used the press to forcefully and passionately speak out against an institution that enslaved millions of black men, women, and children. At a time when most mainstream newspapers in the country either supported slavery or ignored the controversial subject, abolitionist publications provided an editorial platform for the movement's leaders, publicized the work of antislavery societies, and spread news about the treatment of blacks in the South. They helped keep the issue of slavery before the public through the Civil War, when the institution was constitutionally ended by the Thirteenth Amendment.

That abolitionists would use the press as a tool to fight slavery was hardly surprising. Newspaper editors enjoyed a tradition of freedom of expression in the young nation, as guaranteed by the First Amendment. Although that freedom was not always respected by opponents who sometimes used violence to silence journals, government leaders generally kept their hands off newspapers. Since the country's founding, the press had also been intensely aggressive and partisan. Not only had patriot leaders used newspapers to implore the colonists to break from Great Britain, but the press was used by the country's early political parties to campaign for their candidates and attack their opponents. Finally, at the beginning of the nineteenth century, a well-established reform press emerged in the United States. Religious, temperance, and other groups, determined to improve society, used newspapers to spread their messages and attract new followers.

Certainly abolitionist leaders believed that the press was an invaluable tool in the fight against slavery. "Types are potent implements of modern political and moral warfare," declared Benjamin Lundy, editor of one of the first antislavery newspapers, the *Genius of Universal Emancipation.* "Castles fall before them—cannons are silenced." In the first issue of *Freedom's Journal,* the founders wrote: "We deem it expedient to establish a paper, and bring into operation all the means with which our benevolent creator has endowed us, for the moral, religious, civil and literary improvement of our injured race. Experience teaches us that the Press is the most economic and convenient method by which this object is to be obtained." And James Birney, founder of the *Philanthropist,* wrote of the press: "Demagogues and slaveholders may dread its influence and tremble at its power, but the friends of rational liberty and public virtue will cherish it as *the surest safeguard of a free government.*" Such views help explain why an estimated thirty to forty abolitionist publications were founded between 1820 and 1865. Their ranks included such prominent and long-running newspapers as the *Liberator, Philanthropist, National Era, National Anti-Slavery Standard,* and *North Star,* as well as many lesser-known and short-lived journals such as the *Elevator, Mirror of the Times, Mystery, National Watchman, Radical Abolitionist,* and *True American.*[1]

The target of their outrage had become a firmly entrenched institution in the United States by the early nineteenth century. Black slaves were first brought to America in the late seventeenth century, and the use of slave labor became common throughout the American colonies. As the economy of New England became more sophisticated, slave labor was adapted to manufacturing, though slaveholding was never essential to that region's economy. Moreover, the population of blacks there was only a small fraction of the white population.

It was far different in the South, where an agricultural economy depended heavily on slave labor, especially the large plantations where cotton, tobacco, and rice were grown. The invention of the cotton gin in 1793 made slavery enormously profitable in the cultivation of cotton. The cotton grown in the South furnished three-fourths of the world's supply, and by 1840 the South had the most formidable slave economy in the Western world. Of the approximately 3.9 million slaves living in the United States in 1860, one-half lived in the cotton states. However, the great majority of slave owners in the South were small farmers growing staple crops. In fact, an estimated 88 percent of all slaveholders in 1860 owned less than twenty slaves.

The Northern states began to gradually abolish slavery beginning with Vermont in 1777. During the next twenty-seven years, Massachusetts, New Hampshire, Pennsylvania, Rhode Island, Connecticut, New York, and New Jersey all followed suit. At the same time the Northwest Ordinance, based on Thomas Jefferson's plan for organizing the western territories, abolished slavery north of the Ohio and east of the Mississippi rivers, an area which would include the states of Ohio, Indiana, Illinois, Wisconsin, Michigan, and part of Minnesota. However, slavery had many supporters, among them delegates to the Constitutional Convention of 1787. Convention members had no desire to anger the powerful Southern bloc by abolishing slavery. The founding fathers also believed in the sanctity of private property and were not about to take that away, even if the property was human beings. The founders avoided the term *slaves* in the Constitution, but counted them as "three fifths of other persons" for the purposes of taxation and representation in Congress. The Constitution outlawed the importation of slaves after 1808, but it also affirmed the right of owners to recover runaway slaves.

The Quakers were the first group to take a public stand against slavery. Several Quaker leaders, most notably the talented writer John Woolman, published tracts attacking the institution. The first organized society against slavery was founded by Quakers in 1775, and it was incorporated later under the kind of long title that was characteristic of early groups: the Pennsylvania Society for Promoting the Abolition of Slavery, the Relief of Free Negroes Unlawfully Held in Bondage, and for Improving the Condition of the African Race. Other antislavery societies were later organized in New York, Connecticut, New Jersey, Delaware, Maryland, and Virginia. In 1794 delegates from five of these groups met in Philadelphia to form a national organization, the American Convention for Promoting the Abolition of Slavery and Improving the Condition of the African Race.

Despite their good intentions, the early opponents of slavery had little impact. The mere fact that they did not arouse more opposition was one measure of their ineffectualness. They also competed with the efforts of the American Colonization Society, which was founded in 1816 to resettle free blacks in Africa and encourage voluntary emancipation of slaves. The leaders of the society believed that colonization was the best solution to claims that freeing slaves would cause a host of societal and economic problems. With support from the federal government, the colony of Liberia was set up on the West African coast, and in 1820 the first shipload of eighty-eight colonists departed for Africa. Critics of colonization, including many free blacks, argued that colonization was not the answer to the problem of slavery and was little more than a racist scheme concocted by whites to serve their own interests. But colonization also had many supporters who argued that blacks would be better off in Africa, where they would be free from the discrimination they faced in the United States.

At the same time the American Colonization Society was beginning its work, a wave of Protestant revivals sought to reawaken the religious spirit of the country. Led by Lyman Beecher and Charles Finney, powerful evangelists urged their audiences to not only strive for holiness but also assume personal responsibility for helping to reform society. These men of God insisted that the "saved" must serve Christ's kingdom by performing acts of benevolence for a country mired in sin. Reformers tackled myriad issues including temperance, health, women's rights, and education reform. However, for many reformers there was no greater national sin than slavery. In their view, all people were equal in the eyes of God, and for one human being to enslave another was a violation of the creator's laws.

Certainly this view was held by abolitionist editors. Some came to their position as experienced printers or writers. Others had a background in the trades or business, or as a lecturer or minister. In any case, an abolitionist editor quickly had to become a jack-of-all-trades because his small publication demanded that he handle many different tasks. A typical editor's duties ranged from writing editorials and answering letters to setting the type and running the press. The days were long and the pay poor. In 1845 *Emancipator* editor Joshua Leavitt related his precarious financial condition to readers. Leavitt said his home was heavily mortgaged, he walked the two miles to work because he could not afford a horse, and he still used the watch that his father had given him thirty years earlier.[2]

The hard work did not guarantee success. Many abolitionist publications, begun with little financial support and a small circulation base, ceased publishing after only a few years. Even the best-managed newspapers struggled financially because few people were willing to support a radical publication. And virtually all antislavery journals suffered at the hands of a conservative citizenry who often did not like what they advocated and tried to silence them, sometimes with violence. From 1830 to 1860 some two dozen acts of violence were directed at abolitionist publications, and one editor was killed by a mob determined to prevent him from publishing.

None of that mattered to the men and women who considered their antislavery work a calling and believed that what they were doing editorially could make a profound difference in the lives of millions of enslaved blacks. Soon after he had started the *Genius of Universal Emancipation,* skeptics asked Lundy if he thought he could find enough antislavery material to fill up his newspaper. The usually mild-mannered Quaker editor replied scornfully. "If these people had thought *one fourth* of as much as I have upon the subject of slavery," he wrote, "they would never *think* of asking such a question as that."[3]

As I began studying the abolitionist period, it became clear that no published work had examined the role of the antislavery press as a whole. Although there are many noteworthy studies of various aspects of the abolitionist era—including several excellent biographies of antislavery editors—no work has tried to make sense of what these editors and their publications as a group tried and, in many cases, managed to accomplish. Whatever this book's merits or shortcomings, that has been the goal.

As a work of historical synthesis and analysis, this book would not have been possible if not for the many talented scholars whose work it draws upon. In particular I owe a tremendous debt to Merton L. Dillon, Louis Filler, Philip S. Foner, Stanley Harrold, Henry Mayer, James M. McPherson, Russel B. Nye, Benjamin Quarles, James Brewer Stewart, and John L. Thomas. I have tried to fully credit their work—as well as that of other scholars—and I trust I have succeeded.

This book also makes great use of the key abolitionist publications of the era. For their help in locating copies of these newspapers in various formats, as well as the cover illustration, I am grateful to the staff of the Penn State Library, particularly Barb Woods of the Interlibrary Loan Borrowing department and Debora Cheney, Foster Communications Librarian and head of the News and Microforms Library.

I would like to thank David Abrahamson, editor of the Visions of the American Press series, for entrusting me with this project and for his thoughtful guidance during its various stages of work. I am grateful to Penn State for granting me a sabbatical in order to write the initial manuscript and to Dean Doug Anderson of the College of Communications for his encouragement and support. My graduate assistant, Shawnee McFarland, helped track down some of the editorials used. My wife, Mary, and our daughters, Emily and Megan, have supported my work on this book in many ways, both big and small. I can never thank them enough for their love—as well as their patience. Finally, I owe a tremendous debt to my parents. They not only instilled in me an appreciation of history but have always encouraged my academic pursuits. I dedicate this book to them.

ABOLITION AND THE PRESS

ONE

BEGINNINGS OF THE ABOLITIONIST PRESS

On January 1, 1821, a small, four-page newspaper with a lofty title came off a hand press in the Quaker settlement of Mount Pleasant, Ohio. The *Genius of Universal Emancipation* was published by an unassuming harness maker, Benjamin Lundy, who knew little about publishing a newspaper. But that lack of experience did not matter to Lundy, who declared the time had come "to arouse and awaken the American people to a sense of the inconsistency, the hypocrisy, and the iniquity of which many of them are chargeable" because they tolerated the institution of slavery. He promised to make his newspaper "an active instrument in the attempt to abolish that cruel and disgraceful system."[1]

Lundy was not the first to publish a newspaper declaring a mission to oppose slavery, but he became the early antislavery movement's best-known editor. More than any other reform editor in the 1820s, Lundy recognized that a fiery, outspoken publication could be one of the most important tools in opposing slavery in the United States. He laid the foundation for the country's antislavery press and influenced other editors, most notably the young William Lloyd Garrison, to start their own abolitionist publications.

Lundy founded the *Genius* just as the American Colonization Society was beginning its controversial mission of establishing colonies for blacks, and as the Missouri Compromise focused the nation's attention on the spread of slavery into the new territories west of the Mississippi River. With only a small readership, the *Genius* could never claim to be tremendously influential. But as one of the earliest antislavery newspapers, it provided an unmistakable voice of outrage against the institution. Lundy developed antislavery arguments and refined propaganda techniques in his newspaper. Although Lundy's editorial voice would be eclipsed by Garrison before the end of the decade, Garrison and others recognized the great debt they owed to the pioneering Quaker.

Beginning in the early nineteenth century, opposition to slavery emerged in parts of the non-slaveholding upper South and the newly settled west. Residents with no economic stake in slavery, but who had relocated to plantation areas, were generally free to speak out against the institution. Many were Quakers who moved from Pennsylvania to Tennessee and North Carolina. Among the Friends was Charles Osborn, a Quaker minister who settled in Jefferson County, Tennessee, and helped organize an antislavery group that became known as the Tennessee Manumission Society. Two years later, Osborn moved across the border to the nearby community of Mount Pleasant, Ohio. On August 29, 1817, Osborn began publishing the *Philanthropist,* a weekly journal of "such religious, moral, agricultural, and manufacturing information, as may tend to the great aim of giving 'ardour to virtue and confidence to truth.'" Scattered among the practical articles in the publication were antislavery essays and news of manumission societies. Among the volunteers who wrote articles for the *Philanthropist* was Lundy.[2]

Lundy was born in Sandwich, New Jersey, to Quaker parents. His great-grandfather was a founder of the Society of Friends in Bucks County, Pennsylvania, and his family passed down to him an unyielding opposition to slavery. Slight and unassuming with thinning red hair, Lundy's appearance gave no suggestion of his boldness. At the age of twenty he moved to Wheeling, Virginia (now West Virginia), and apprenticed himself to a saddler to learn harness making. There he witnessed chains of black men and women put on boats to be sent south. Lundy later wrote that he was shocked by the sight of slaves "chained together and driven through the streets, *bare-headed* and *bare-footed, in mud and snow,* by the remorseless 'SOUL SELLERS.'" At that moment, he made a solemn vow to God that he would "break at least one link of that ponderous chain of oppression." The young Quaker eventually moved to Mount Pleasant and helped organize the Union Humane Society. The group declared that its goals were to end racial prejudice, help freed blacks become productive members of society, and work toward the gradual emancipation of the nation's slaves.[3]

Under Osborn's direction, the *Philanthropist* gradually became more of a general interest publication. The newspaper still opposed slavery, but that message was often lost in material on other subjects. In the meantime, another abolitionist publication appeared, the *Emancipator,* sponsored by the Tennessee Manumission Society and published by Elihu Embree. Embree was the son of a Quaker minister who had moved from Pennsylvania to Tennessee as a young man. Embree had an iron-manufacturing business with his brother and had even owned a few slaves as a young man. However, he freed his slaves in 1812 and became a devoted antislavery worker.[4]

Writing in the *Emancipator,* Embree brooked no words in describing slaveholders as "monsters in human shape." The editor used his newspaper to warn that, if continued, slavery would "produce such scenes of misery and destruction for our posterity . . . as have not been exceeded in the history of man." Embree viewed slaves as "prisoners of war" and predicted violence would eventually break out as slaves sought to break the chains binding them. He portrayed opponents of slavery as "mediators between the oppressor and the oppressed" who tried to avert violence by promoting emancipation. When congressional leaders agreed to the controversial Missouri Compromise, a furious Embree wrote, "Hell is about to enlarge her borders; and tyranny her domain." Unhappy with what the editor wrote, opponents tried to stop distribution of the paper by opening the mails and destroying copies of it. It mattered little, however, because the *Emancipator* lasted less than a year. Embree died suddenly on December 6, 1820, at the age of thirty-eight, leaving no one to continue publishing the paper.[5]

Lundy, who had been reading the *Emancipator,* believed that the brash and outspoken journal was just what a true abolitionist publication should be, and he moved quickly to start a similar paper in 1821. He took the title for the *Genius of Universal Emancipation* from a phrase the Irish orator John Philpot Curran had used in an eloquent defense of a man accused of seditious libel. It did not matter that Lundy had no money, no press, and no subscribers. The greenhorn editor saw himself following in the grand tradition of resistance to oppression and injustice. With little help, Lundy found printers wherever he could, regularly traveling to nearby Steubenville and often on foot.

While waiting for the type to be set, he sometimes worked at his old trade of harness maker to pay the cost of printing the newspaper.[6]

Lundy was far from a gentle Quaker in his descriptions of slaveholders. In one editorial, he called them "too depraved to blush, and too wicked to repent." In another he called slave owners "ipso facto the most disgraceful whoremongers upon earth; they make a *business* of raising bastards and selling them for money." He occasionally published a "Black List" of horrific treatment of slaves by their owners. He also printed the views of other writers who called slave owners "monsters in human shape," "blood suckers," and "miserable sons of avarice." To those who objected to such harsh language, Lundy said that slaveholders "must be addressed in such language as will reach their adamantine hearts."[7]

However, the editor was not just interested in condemning slaveholders. He used the *Genius* to examine ways of abolishing slavery. Most opponents of the institution during this time called for the gradual end of slavery, and Lundy could be counted in this group. Like other supporters of "gradualism," Lundy did not argue for the immediate emancipation of all slaves. He sought change with the least possible disturbance to the social order. Lundy said he was realistic enough to recognize that full emancipation would probably not happen in his lifetime. He constantly preached patience, believing time would remedy many evils.[8]

At the same time, Lundy argued that the federal government should abolish slavery in all the western territories and prohibit the admission of any new slave states to the Union. He also believed that the interstate slave trade should be ended immediately. Lundy maintained that political action was the only way to achieve results. "I don't expect to 'persuade' the advocates of slavery to do justice," he wrote. "Such persons cannot be honest; and I am not for making a covenant with dishonesty."[9]

Many of Lundy's arguments against slavery came from the Bible, particularly Old Testament prophecies that God would punish those on earth who defied his laws. On a secular level, he and others argued that slavery violated the rights guaranteed in the Declaration of Independence and a republican government in general. "Humanitas" called upon churchmen to fight against slavery. He maintained that "if 'life, liberty and pursuit of Happiness' are undeniable rights of man; if 'all the nations of men who dwell upon the earth are created of one blood'; if all are sons of one common father, and equally objects of a Redeemer's love; let the professors of Christianity arise from their thoughtless lethargy."[10]

The *Genius* provided a forum for other writers to express their views on slavery. A writer from Pennsylvania argued that "had the British parliament advocated the gradual abolition of the slave trade, it would not yet have been accomplished, for by the same reasoning that slavery could be proved to be right for a single day, by the very same reasoning it could be proved to be right for a year or forever." Another writer claimed that "it is not our province to reason whether we shall obey the commands of justice, or not—but it is our bounden duty and high privilege to comply immediately, reckless of consequences."[11]

In early 1822 Lundy moved the *Genius* to Greeneville, a small town in eastern Tennessee. There the paper could be printed on the press of the Tennessee Manumission Society while Lundy learned the printing trade. By publishing in a slave state, Lundy also believed the *Genius* would serve an important purpose in symbolizing opposition to the institution. Not surprisingly, the editor soon found himself repeatedly "threatened in various ways." But the attacks proved to be mere words, and no violence accompanied them.[12]

The early antislavery movement in the United States was largely disorganized and uncoordinated. While antislavery societies had been started in many places, most were small, local groups that sponsored occasional meetings but few other activities. The *Genius* had no official connection with any organization, although it regularly published the reports of antislavery societies in Tennessee, North Carolina, and Kentucky. Without financial support from any sponsoring antislavery society, the *Genius* struggled mightily. The income from the newspaper's small number of subscribers barely kept Lundy and his family fed and clothed.

The only national antislavery organization of any kind was the American Convention for Promoting the Abolition of Slavery. Lundy hoped the organization would agree to sponsor the *Genius,* and in 1823 he traveled on horseback to Philadelphia to attend the group's annual meeting. Convention members formally recognized Lundy's contribution to the antislavery movement and appointed him to two important committees, but the group decided it was not in a financial position to support a publication. Although disappointed, Lundy left Philadelphia convinced that if the *Genius* was ever going to be successful, he needed to move the newspaper to the country's centers of wealth and political power. Leaving his wife and children behind in Tennessee, he traveled by foot to Baltimore, where he set up shop in 1824.[13]

In Baltimore Lundy became a supporter of a new plan to encourage blacks to immigrate to Haiti. Since colonial times, various proposals had been put forth to establish a colony for blacks from the United States. The growing number of free blacks prompted more calls to help a population that some believed would always be barred from voting and serving on juries, not to mention dining in restaurants or sitting in church pews with whites. Supporters of colonization believed that it was far better for the federal government to establish settlements in Africa and elsewhere, places where blacks could immigrate to and lead a better life. In 1816 delegates from several states met in Washington, D.C., and organized the American Colonization Society. However, many free blacks opposed colonization, arguing that it violated American principles and countenanced slavery by removing free blacks. By the 1820s, only a few hundred blacks had emigrated.[14]

Lundy believed that the climate and nearness of Haiti to the United States made it far more attractive to blacks than Africa. He dismissed critics who claimed the Haiti plan was merely designed to keep blacks from living permanently in the United States. Blacks had every right to live in the country, Lundy wrote, but he believed supporters of emancipation also had to recognize that "prejudice too often presents itself to us as an insurmountable barrier to the attainment of happiness." Realistic people should agree that the discrimination blacks faced in the United States meant that in many cases they would be better off in a place where they could enjoy social and legal equality. The editor believed that slavery could not realistically be brought to an end for at least a century, and by that time an estimated three million blacks would be living in the country. With so many people enslaved, Lundy envisioned racial warfare like that which had taken place in Santo Domingo. Freeing blacks and transporting them to Haiti would effectively reduce the slave population. It would also ease the understandable racial anger of blacks in the United States until all slaves could be emancipated, he claimed.[15]

Lundy used the *Genius* to publicize the few cases of slaveholders who freed their slaves and sent them to Haiti. He also printed letters from Haitian settlers who had found emigration there to be worthwhile. Lundy continued to tout immigration even after the Haitian government ended financial support for the program, and it became apparent that a relatively small number of freed slaves had been sent to the country. He even traveled to Haiti in an effort to persuade government officials to reverse their decision.

While he was in Haiti, Lundy's wife died during childbirth. He returned to Baltimore to find his five children living with various people. Deciding he could not properly care for his offspring, Lundy arranged for relatives and friends to take care of them on a permanent basis. The editor now dedicated his life to the antislavery cause. Lundy had been criticized by some for traveling to Haiti while his wife was pregnant, but the attacks were nothing new. His harsh language and unceasing criticism of slavery had made him unpopular with many. However, the condemnation did not bother Lundy, who always maintained he answered to a higher calling. "Ours is the cause of Justice; it is the Cause of Heaven," he wrote in the *Genius*. "No earthly consideration should interfere with it."[16]

In Baltimore, Lundy lived among slaveholders and slaves. The thriving port city was a center of slave trading, and the practice horrified the editor, who used the *Genius* to repeatedly criticize slave trading. Among his most prominent targets was the Woolfolk family, one of Maryland's leading slave traders. In January 1826, Austin Woolfolk was transporting twenty-nine slaves from Baltimore to Georgia when the slaves mutinied, threw the captain overboard, and sailed for Haiti, where they hoped to find safe harbor. Another ship overtook the muti-neers and escorted them to New York. Upon arriving, all the slaves managed to escape except William Bowser. He was tried and convicted of mutiny and murder. In a farewell speech from the gallows, Bowser forgave Woolfolk for being a slave trader. Woolfolk was unrepentant, however, and reportedly cursed Bowser.

Lundy reported the story in the *Genius,* calling Woolfolk a "monster." For his part, the slave trader denied being present at Bowser's hanging. A few days later, Woolfolk confronted Lundy on the street and accused the editor of libeling him. Woolfolk knocked Lundy to the pavement and beat him repeat-edly until bystanders pulled him away. At his trial for assault, Woolfolk pleaded guilty to the charge but claimed he had been provoked by Lundy's inflammatory articles in the *Genius.* His lawyers read excerpts in which Lundy called Woolfolk a "soul seller" and denounced the slave trade as "barbarous, inhuman and unchristian." The judge found Woolfolk guilty but, in a clear slap at Lundy, fined the slave trader only one dollar and court costs. The judge also commented that he "had never seen a case in which the provocation for a battery was greater," and said the editor was mistaken in calling the slave trade evil when, in fact, it was an important part of the state's economy. With the judge's encouragement, Woolfolk brought charges of libel against Lundy, but a grand jury refused to indict him. Lundy clearly was finding the South a difficult place in which to publish an abolitionist newspaper.[17]

Lundy sparked controversy in Baltimore once again when he drafted a petition to Congress requesting the gradual abolition of slavery in the District of Columbia. The petition was not new;

similar petitions had been received for decades from Quakers and other critics who argued that permitting slavery in the nation's capital implied federal support for the institution. However, Lundy's petition went farther. Written in the editor's characteristically strong language, the petition condemned slavery as a violation of republican and Christian principles. When Lundy reprinted the petition in the *Genius,* it caused an uproar in the city. Even some supporters of colonization questioned what they considered Lundy's extreme views. Congressmen, including a representative from Maryland, angrily criticized the petition, and the House of Representatives voted not to even print it.[18]

At the same time that Lundy was facing increasing criticism in Baltimore for his outspoken views, Samuel Cornish and John Russwurm, two young free blacks in New York City, were starting a new antislavery publication, one not seen before. On March 16, 1827, the two men launched *Freedom's Journal,* the first black-owned newspaper in the United States. Cornish, born in Delaware to free blacks, had founded the first black Presbyterian church in New York—the First Colored Presbyterian Church. Russwurm, born in Jamaica to a white American plantation owner and a black woman, was one of the first nonwhites to graduate from a college in the United States. Although it is not clear what brought the two men together, black leaders in New York had been concerned about what they considered racist and disparaging portrayals of blacks in a variety of publications. Newspapers in the city frequently printed sensationalized accounts of crimes by blacks. Satirical broadsides and cartoons, widely circulated, portrayed blacks as unrefined fools who were unable to act as respectable citizens. "We wish to plead our own cause," Cornish and Russwurm declared in the first issue. "Too long have others spoken for us. Too long has the publick been deceived by misrepresentations, in things which concern us dearly."[19]

Although Cornish and Russwurm opposed slavery, the editors made clear that *Freedom's Journal*'s chief goal was to be an advocate for the free blacks of the North. They believed that blacks must be able to publicly speak for themselves in order to dispel misrepresentations of the race held by most whites. "Daily slandered, we think there ought to be some channel of communion between us and the publick, through which a single voice may be heard, in defense of five hundred thousand free people of colour," the editors wrote. "For often has injustice been heaped upon us when our only defense was an appeal to the Almighty; but we believe that the time has now arrived, when the calumnies of our enemies should be refuted by forcible arguments."[20]

Freedom's Journal was meant to be, in the words of one historian of the publication, "living proof that black persons had the potential for intellectual and cultural achievement." Cornish and Russwurm published biographical sketches of successful black Americans. They printed obituaries of blacks, which often took the form of tributes to the deceased. The editors also made the newspaper a lively forum for black leaders who contributed articles and speeches on religious, educational, political, and scientific topics.[21]

In the paper's first issue, Cornish and Russwurm declared they wanted to improve the moral and religious character of blacks in order to gain the acceptance of white society. The editors and their contributors constantly promoted education, arguing it was the best way for blacks to advance financially and socially. A contributor known as "Amicus" wrote in 1827: "Let the People of Colour, who would call themselves their own masters, join heart and hand in the work of *education*, and suffer nothing, absolutely *nothing*, for themselves and *their* children, to rival the subject of useful knowledge and right education." Amicus said readers should take control of their own education, rather than wait for others to provide opportunities. *Freedom's Journal* also repeatedly criticized the poor educational facilities provided for the race and said blacks should speak out in protest.[22]

The newspaper's slogan was "Righteousness Exalteth a Nation," and although *Freedom's Journal* spoke out against slavery, the editors were vague about any action that should be taken against the institution. No doubt, they were also concerned that a black-owned publication that spoke out too forcefully against slavery would be subject to violence. "We would not be unmindful of our brethren who are still in the iron fetters of bondage," Cornish and Russwurm wrote in the first issue. "They are our kindred by all the times of nature; and though but little can be effected by us, still let our sympathies be poured forth." The newspaper printed news accounts of the horrors of slavery, including the brutal killing of blacks at the hands of their masters. It also published reports on the slave trade, trying to show the human cost of the practice.[23]

Both editors initially opposed colonization efforts, and *Freedom's Journal* published articles and letters criticizing the work of the American Colonization Society. Contributors argued that colonization strengthened prejudice against blacks and weakened the goal of emancipation. They argued that many of the society's members viewed blacks as "an inferior race" solely because of the color of their skin. One contributor wrote: "Any plan which implies in our brethren or their descendants, inferiority, or carries with it the idea that they cannot be raised to respectable standing in this country . . . is wholly at war with our best interests, and we cannot view the Advocates of such sentiments, in any other light, than that of enemies, whatever their principles may be." However, Russwurm soon began to support the society, arguing that colonization was the best solution to the slavery issue. Prejudice had existed against blacks for so long in America, he wrote in one issue, that "we are bold in saying, that it will never be in our power to remove or overcome" it. Cornish, on the other hand, refused to support colonization. Although historians disagree, some believe the colonization issue led him to quit, just six months after *Freedom's Journal* was founded.[24]

Russwurm tried to keep the newspaper alive. He printed works by black poets and republished popular works by black writers, including Othello's "An Essay on Negro Slavery" and James Forten's "A Series of Letters by a Man of Color." Russwurm also continued urging blacks to improve their condition in society. He decried the "evil actions" of some free blacks, which he said brought the "whole body into disgrace" in the eyes of white Americans. He encouraged readers to "be up & doing," making it clear that this should not be accessory to the work of benevolent whites. He also maintained that as black Americans organized to advocate self-help, they promoted advancement of the race. At the same time, Russwurm continued arguing for support of the American Colonization Society. The editor was now convinced that blacks in the United States would never be able to achieve equality with whites "for certain reasons which are known and felt daily." "We consider it mere waste of words to talk of ever enjoying citizenship in this country," Russwurm wrote in another issue. "It is utterly impossible in the nature of things; all therefore who pant for these, must cast their eyes elsewhere."[25]

However, Russwurm received a great deal of criticism for his support of colonization. Some believed he had been co-opted by the American Colonization Society, a charge he denied. In any case, an angry and bitter Russwurm quit the paper in 1829. In his final editorial, he expressed pessimism for the future of black Americans. "If we cast our eyes at home, in our own land, or abroad, in foreign lands, we find no people exactly situated as we are—we find none so low and degraded—so dead to all the noble feelings which actuate intelligent and immortal beings," he wrote. "What is still worse, we see no probability, that we as a community, will ever make it our earnest endeavor to rise from our ignorance and degradation." Russwurm later moved to Liberia and went on to become the superintendent of schools there, as well as the editor of the *Liberia Herald*.[26]

With Russwurm gone, Cornish returned and changed the name of the newspaper to the *Rights of All*. He continued to promote the moral and educational advancement of blacks. He encouraged qualified blacks to vote, and he criticized New York for its law requiring only blacks to take a qualification test in order to vote. He also renewed his attacks on colonization. However, with few subscribers and little outside financial support, *Rights of All* ceased publishing before the end of 1829.[27]

The first black-owned newspapers had gotten off to an inauspicious start—and indeed they were hardly the sharpest critics of slavery. Nonetheless, *Freedom's Journal* and *Rights of All* were significant in providing a valuable editorial forum for free blacks. Not only did Cornish and Russwurm establish a platform to express their views, but the two men published material from a wide variety of black writers, writers who otherwise would have found no place for their work. In doing so, they inspired many other free blacks to start their own publications, some of which would be far more critical of slavery.

By 1827, the circulation of the *Genius of Universal Emancipation* still numbered less than a thousand. Although Lundy had managed to secure some donations from antislavery groups, the journal was barely able to pay its bills. Lundy saw New England as a fertile source of new subscribers to the *Genius*. In 1828 the editor left on a tour of the region, where he planned to make antislavery speeches and drum up support for his newspaper. After making stops in New York City and Providence, where he found no backing for the *Genius,* Lundy traveled to Boston, the cultural and religious center of New England. There he stayed at the boardinghouse of William Collier, a local Baptist clergyman and the founder of the *National Philanthropist,* a journal of universal reform.

Also staying at the boardinghouse was William Lloyd Garrison, a pious young man from Newburyport, Massachusetts, who was editing the *Philanthropist.* Garrison had been reading the *Genius,* and when Lundy gave a talk to a group of Boston clergymen, he was in the audience. As Garrison wrote years later, he had imagined the editor to be Herculean in size and was disappointed to find him small and generally unimpressive. Nonetheless, he was captivated by Lundy's dedication to the antislavery cause and afterward introduced himself. Garrison told Lundy of his admiration for his newspaper and showed him an editorial he had written warning of "a national catastrophe" if slavery was not ended. Over the next several months, Lundy and Garrison exchanged letters. It soon became clear to Garrison that Lundy was a role model for the kind of ardent and outspoken reform editor he wanted to be.[28]

Garrison had grown up in poverty in Newburyport, a town of five thousand residents on the Atlantic coast. His father was a seaman who was constantly out of work and drank heavily. After a fight with his wife, he left the family when Garrison was only three years old. The family he left behind was penniless and struggled for years. As a young boy, Garrison sold home-made molasses candy from street corners. His mother often sent him to collect table scraps from the homes of neighbors, and he would trudge back home with the food, listening to the jeers of other children. Garrison's mother was a Baptist and a deeply religious woman. Determined that her three children would not turn out like their father, she raised them to strictly follow the teachings of God. "Oh Lloyd," she wrote to the young Garrison, "if I was to hear and have reason to think you unsteady, it would break my heart. God forbid! You are now at an age when you are forming character for life, a dangerous age. Shun every appearance of evil for the sake of your soul as well as the body."[29]

Garrison's mother did not have to worry because he was a dutiful, serious-minded son. When he was thirteen, Garrison was apprenticed to the editor of the *Newburyport Herald*. Garrison learned the printing business quickly, and by the time he was seventeen he had become shop foreman. The young man continued to attend church regularly and sing in the choir. He also read constantly and, with a growing number of friends, discussed the issues of the day, including slavery.

When he turned twenty, Garrison's apprenticeship ended and he left the *Herald*. He remained in Newburyport and became editor of the *Newburyport Free Press,* a short-lived Federalist Party paper. While editor, he began printing the works of John

Greenleaf Whittier, a young Quaker whose poems about helping mankind through Christian service appealed to Garrison. But by the end of the year, the *Free Press* was forced to close and Garrison moved to Boston. For a year, he moved from one printing shop in the city to another. Then he met Collier, who was editing the struggling *National Philanthropist*. The reform paper denounced the evils of alcohol, gambling, and prostitution while extolling the virtues of Christian faith. Garrison was named editor of the paper in January 1828. Under his direction, the journal campaigned for moral reform with evangelical zeal, but it rarely discussed the subject of slavery.

After meeting Lundy, Garrison wrote a lengthy editorial lauding the *Genius* and its editor. He boldly proclaimed the little newspaper "the bravest and best attempt" in the history of newspaper publishing, and described its editor as a Quaker in the mold of William Penn. Garrison also praised Lundy's Haitian colonization plan, arguing that many blacks had successfully emigrated to the island and found a better life. For his part, Lundy returned to Baltimore to face the same problems he had when he left on his tour. When he was unable to pay his bills in the fall of 1828, creditors took most of his printing equipment, and the editor was forced to suspend the *Genius* for several months. During this time, Lundy proposed to Garrison that he move to Baltimore and join the *Genius*. Garrison would become editor of the newspaper, freeing Lundy to lecture and work on behalf of Haitian colonization. Garrison eagerly agreed.[30]

The first issue of the *Genius* with Garrison's name on the masthead appeared on September 2, 1829. The newspaper was now a weekly, and it boasted a new flag and improved typeface. Beneath an American eagle on the masthead were words from the Declaration of Independence proclaiming the equality of all men. Lundy announced in this issue that he would spend most of his time traveling to organize antislavery societies and find subscribers for the *Genius,* while Garrison edited the paper in Baltimore. Both men would write editorials.[31]

By the time he moved to Baltimore, Garrison had begun to have serious reservations about colonization. Although he believed the American Colonization Society had the best interests of blacks at heart, emigration was not the answer to slavery. "The work of colonization is exceedingly dilatory and uncertain," he wrote in the *Genius.* "Viewed as an auxiliary, it deserves encouragement, but as a remedy, it is altogether inadequate . . . if we depend alone upon the efforts of the colonization societies, slavery will never be exterminated." Garrison now believed that nothing short of total and immediate emancipation was right for slaves. He declared that "no valid excuse can be given for the continuance of the evil a single hour."[32]

Under Garrison's direction, the *Genius* condemned slavery even more harshly than before. The young editor revived the "Black List" started by Lundy. He stepped up editorial criticism of the Woolfolk family's slave-trading enterprises, even issuing a public challenge to Austin Woolfolk to meet if he wished to complain about the criticism published by the *Genius.* "Let me assure him," Garrison wrote, "that I am not to be intimidated by the utterances of any threats, or the perpetration of any violence." He also criticized the *Baltimore American* for carrying Woolfolk's advertisements.[33]

The combative Garrison also took sharp aim at slave traders elsewhere. When he heard that the *Francis,* a slave ship owned by Francis Todd of Massachusetts, had left Baltimore for New Orleans with seventy-five slaves on board, he called it "domestic piracy." He denounced men like Todd as "enemies of their own species—highway robbers and murderers." He went on: "Any man can gather up riches if he does not care by what means they are obtained." With characteristic bluster, Garrison even mailed Todd a copy of the article just to make sure he saw it. The slave trader promptly filed suit against Garrison and Lundy, seeking $5,000 for damages to his reputation. A Baltimore grand jury took just fifteen minutes to indict the two men for "gross and malicious libel." The judge threw out the indictment against Lundy because he was out of town when the article was published. However, Garrison was fined fifty dollars or six months in jail. Unable to pay the fine, Garrison was locked up.[34]

While in jail, Garrison wrote his own account of the trial, which he published in an eight-page pamphlet. He defended the principles of a free press and argued that the Baltimore court had conducted "a burlesque upon the Constitution." Garrison also declared that the conviction would not keep him from continuing to use the press to fight against slavery. "So long as a good providence gives me strength and intellect, I will not cease to declare that the existence of slavery is a foul reproach to the American name," he wrote. After forty-nine days behind bars, Lundy secured Garrison's release by paying his fine. Arthur Tappan, a wealthy businessman and philanthropist from New York, had read Garrison's account of the trial and sent $150 to pay the fine and keep the *Genius* publishing. It marked the beginning of a long, but often fractious relationship between Garrison and Tappan.[35]

By this time it was clear to Lundy that publishing an antislavery paper on a weekly basis was not financially doable. The journal's expenses were running at least fifty dollars a week, and the *Genius* was not making nearly that much from subscription sales. Lundy announced that he was dissolving the partnership with Garrison and making the *Genius* a monthly once again. Lundy made clear that the parting was amicable and not the result of any disagreement with Garrison. He praised his young coeditor for "his strict integrity, amiable deportment, and virtuous conduct."[36]

While locked away, Garrison had begun thinking about starting his own antislavery newspaper. He and Lundy enjoyed a good working relationship, but Garrison wanted total editorial license. That was impossible with Lundy because of his unwavering support for colonization. While in jail, Garrison had written three exposés about colonization, and he decided to deliver them during a lecture tour. He also hoped that the tour to Philadelphia, New York, and Boston would raise money for the new antislavery publication. On the tour, Garrison's audiences included future abolitionist leaders such as Samuel May, Lucretia Mott, Lyman Beecher, and Bronson Alcott. Most praised the young man's call to end slavery immediately, but they also rebuked him for his harsh language. Garrison refused to back down. "That is a providential man," May remembered later telling an acquaintance. When May tried to warn Garrison about the harshness of his rhetoric, Garrison replied, "Brother May, I have need to be on fire, for I have mountains of ice about me to melt."[37]

Garrison considered several cities for his newspaper, but he eventually settled on Boston after audiences in several other New England cities had turned down his lecture on colonization. He had become convinced that there was a greater need for a revolution in public opinion in a part of the country where "the curse of slavery" had been eliminated, but "the curse of deep-rooted prejudice" still existed. He wanted to launch his publication, as he wrote, *"within sight of Bunker Hill and in the birth place of Liberty."* Garrison chose to name his newspaper the *Liberator,* despite the arguments of some that the title was too inflammatory.[38]

When the first issue appeared on New Year's Day 1831, the 25-year-old editor made clear that the *Liberator* would be a frank and uncompromising advocate for the immediate end of slavery. The newspaper's outspoken approach would anger many, he recognized, but he did not care. "I am aware that many object to the severity of my language," he wrote, "but is there not cause for severity?" He went on with words that have become perhaps his most often quoted: "I *will be* as harsh as truth, and as uncompromising as justice. On this subject, I do not wish to think, or speak, or write, with moderation. No! No! . . . I am in earnest—I will not equivocate—I will not excuse—I will not retreat a single inch—AND I WILL BE HEARD."[39]

Week after week, the *Liberator* blasted away at slavery from an office in Merchants' Hall, a four-story building at the corner of Congress and Water streets in the heart of the city. The cramped office with ink-splattered windows housed a used hand press, type cases, composing desk, mailing table, and even a bed where Garrison often slept. With help from a boyhood friend, Isaac Knapp, who was listed as the publisher, Garrison did virtually everything: setting the type, manning the press, compiling mailing lists, answering letters, and writing some of the fieriest editorials ever seen in an American newspaper.

The *Liberator* attacked racial prejudice as strongly as slavery itself. In an early issue Garrison published a list of "truisms" that mocked what he called the contradictions of American society. "If white men are ignorant and depraved, they ought freely to receive the benefits of education," one read, "but if black men are in this condition, common sense dictates that they should be held in bondage and never instructed." Garrison also emphasized the need for the social, economic, and political betterment of black citizens. Racial discrimination in judicial, educational, business, and transportation laws were "gross and palpable violations" of the U.S. Constitution, he argued. Addressing blacks directly, the editor called for political action to challenge "every law which infringes on your rights as free native citizens."[40]

During its first year, the *Liberator* had few subscribers—and many of them were free blacks. Garrison had made black friends while living in Baltimore, and as he traveled, he met many impressive black leaders who confirmed his views about the abilities of the race. He encouraged black writers to pen articles for the newspaper, and they enthusiastically responded. One was Maria W. Stewart, a devout Christian and deeply devoted abolitionist. Garrison showcased Stewart's essays by creating a "Ladies Department"—complete with a woodcut of a black woman in chains—for the *Liberator*. Stewart believed that blacks must fight for their rights, and she encouraged black women to move beyond their limited roles to help lead racial progress.[41]

Garrison also made clever use of newspaper exchanges, a popular practice in which editors around the country swapped newspapers with one another at no cost. The exchange system provided newspapers with stories and editorials from other newspapers in distant locations. Editors merely clipped the articles and published them as written, giving credit to the original newspaper.[42]

Southern editors who received the *Liberator* were outraged at its editorials, but reprinted them to show what they considered to be the North's view of slavery, often adding their own vituperative comments. Garrison would then publish his original editorial with the response and add his comments. As furious letters piled up, Garrison reveled in the notorious reputation he was gaining. "Foes are on my right hand and on my left," he wrote gleefully in one editorial. Above the *Liberator*'s front-page nameplate, he added an elaborate woodcut depicting a slave auction in front of the nation's capitol. The unmistakable image angered more people and even prompted Senator John C. Calhoun of South Carolina to try unsuccessfully to ban newspapers with "pictorial representations" of slavery from the mails.[43]

Critics accused Garrison of condoning violence, as when he discussed an incendiary pamphlet written by David Walker, a black clothier in Boston. The son of a slave father and a free mother from North Carolina, Walker had wandered throughout the South before settling in Boston. Walker had gained a rudimentary education, and he believed history showed that God often intervened to help oppressed races. His pamphlet, popularly known as *Walker's Appeal*, denounced slavery in stark terms and called on slaves to rise up against their masters in a violent mass revolt. "Kill or be killed," he declared. The pamphlet was widely distributed among free blacks in the North and even found its way into the hands of blacks as far south as Georgia. Southerners were outraged. Garrison claimed he did not support the violence that Walker called for, but he argued that Walker was simply doing what the American people should expect by their support of slavery. "Our guilty countrymen . . . put arguments into the mouths, and swords into the hands of the slaves," the editor wrote. "Every sentence that they write—every word that they speak—every resistance that they make, against foreign oppression, is a call upon their slaves to destroy them."[44]

When a slave named Nat Turner heeded Walker's call—and Garrison seemed to gloat over the event—the *Liberator* got the attention its editor wanted. The fanatical Turner believed he had been chosen by God to lead the country's slaves out of bondage. On August 21, 1831, Turner and a large group of blacks from a Virginia plantation in Southampton County armed themselves and went on a murderous rampage, killing fifty-seven whites, including many women and children. Turner's band was easily captured, but the leader managed to elude the state militia for seven weeks. During that time, more than one hundred blacks in Southampton County died at the hands of vigilantes seeking revenge for the rampage.

The "Southampton Tragedy" enraged and alarmed South-erners who had long worried about slave uprisings. Garrison said he did not support violence and insisted that he had no connection with Turner's revolt. But he also argued that the United States, not Turner, was responsible for the bloody insur-rection—as well as the reprisals that followed in which more than a hundred blacks were killed, many after being brutally tortured. Turner and his band had done nothing worse, the editor wrote, "than the Greeks in destroying the Turks, or the Poles in exterminating the Russians, or our fathers in slaugh-tering the British." He also proclaimed that the uprising would in no way stop abolitionists from calling for an end to slavery. "We shall cry, in trumpet tones, night and day—Wo to this guilty land, unless she speedily repent of her evil doings!" he wrote. "The blood of millions of her sons cries aloud for redress! IMMEDIATE EMANCIPATION can alone save her from the vengeance of Heaven, and cancel the debt of ages!"[45]

Outraged critics accused the *Liberator* of inciting slave violence. Garrison received dozens of angry letters, some making death threats. One letter writer said: "You seem to hope to rouse the slave to some act of desperation, but let me assure you that no writing of yours will ever accomplish it—It would require a man of more sense and mettle than yourself—O! you pitiful scoundrel! You toad eater! You d——d son of ——! Hell is gaping for you! The devil is feasting in anticipation!" Some in the press also believed Garrison must be stopped. The editor of Washington's influential *National Intelligencer* called him a "madman" and declared that only a "straight jacket and bread and water" could convince him of the lunacy of his actions. The newspaper called on the mayor of Boston or the legislature of Massachusetts to silence Garrison.[46]

Garrison responded that "the slaves need no incentives at our hands. They will find them in their stripes—in the emaciated bodies—in the ceaseless toil—in their ignorant minds—in every field, in every valley, on every hill-top and mountain." The *Liberator* reported Turner's flight, hiding, and capture over the next several weeks. Garrison also published a special edition with Turner's lengthy confession. And when Turner was executed, the *Liberator* described his composure and bearing on the gallows.[47]

All this was too much for many in the South, and dozens of communities passed legislation with seemingly no thought of First Amendment guarantees. A vigilance committee in Columbia, South Carolina, offered a reward of $1,500 for the capture of any white person caught circulating the *Liberator*. The town of Georgetown in the District of Columbia passed an ordinance prohibiting free blacks from taking copies of the newspaper out of the post office under penalty of a $25 fine and 30 days in jail. (If the fine and jail fees were not paid, the guilty person could be sold into slavery for four months.) And the Georgia legislature passed a resolution offering a $5,000 reward to "any person or persons who shall arrest, bring to trial and prosecute to conviction, under the laws of this state the editor or publisher of a certain paper called the Liberator."[48]

Garrison joked that the $1,500 reward offered by the South Carolina vigilance committee was a "pretty liberal sum. But, without vanity or boasting, we think the numbers of the Liberator are worth more." However, he was outraged by the Georgia reward for anyone who arrested him and brought him to the state to be put on trial. "A bribe to kidnappers, a price set upon the head of a citizen from Massachusetts!" he proclaimed. Garrison used the attacks on the *Liberator* to defend freedom of the press. "Where is the liberty of the press and of speech? Where the spirit of our fathers? Where the immunities secured to us by our Bill of Rights?" he thundered. "Is it treason to maintain the principles of the Declaration of Independence? Must we say that slavery is a sacred and benevolent institution, or be silent? . . . The Liberator shall yet live—live to warn you of your danger and guilt—live to plead for the perishing slave—live to hail the day of universal emancipation."[49]

While Garrison was courting controversy in the *Liberator,* Lundy quietly continued using the *Genius of Universal Emancipation* to work on behalf of the country's blacks. The dogged editor had begun issuing the *Genius* again as a monthly in June 1830. Later that year, he decided to move the paper to Washington, D.C., where he could be closer to the "intelligent and influential men, from every part of the Union." Lundy regularly publicized the worsening condition of free blacks in many places. In some cities, kidnappers roamed the streets grabbing men and women and returning them to slavery. Mobs in Providence, New Haven, Cincinnati, and elsewhere wrecked black homes and businesses. At the same time, Western states passed laws preventing blacks from settling on free soil. The mainstream press often downplayed the violence against free blacks in the North and in some cases defended it.[50]

Some victims of the violence fled into Canada. Wilberforce, a colony named for the famous British abolitionist leader, became a haven for free blacks who left the United States. Lundy touted the Canadian colony in the *Genius* and predicted that soon it would become larger than the American Colonization Society's colony of Liberia. In the summer of 1830, the editor began making plans to visit Wilberforce to see the colony for himself. With little money and no one to publish the *Genius* in his absence, Lundy decided to take the journal with him, stopping in various places where he could find local printers to do the work. Along the way, he would also work at his old trade of harness making to pay the printing expenses. "Thee will, no doubt, smile at the idea of an *itinerant editor!* and probably laugh outright, to think of an *itinerant periodical!!*" he wrote to a friend. "But never mind . . . I will 'continue' many schemes, before I abandon a purpose that I have once resolved on."[51]

Traveling by every means possible, including long stretches on foot, Lundy eventually made it to Wilberforce. Although the editor saw much that he liked in the Canadian outpost, he also found many examples of racial prejudice. After attending meetings in the colony, he learned that blacks there were divided over various issues. Lundy still supported the settlement of blacks in Canada, but after his visit he was more careful in endorsing the idea. "I would not urge, I would not ask a single free man to go, who is not so disposed. My business is to give him information. If he can profit by it I shall rejoice, if he neglects to pay attention to it but exercises a perfect right which it would be highly improper for me to question him about," he wrote later in the

Genius. "I shall be amply rewarded for the hardship and expense of my cold and toilsome journalism, if I can be successful in laying it, generally, before them."[52]

Lundy remained convinced that colonization was the answer to the racial prejudice blacks faced in the United States. On his way back home from Canada, he decided to pursue another place for free blacks to settle: Texas. The idea had been considered by the editor and other supporters of colonization for years. During his trip, Lundy heard from many free blacks who liked the idea. The editor had long argued that in a warm climate, blacks could raise cotton, tobacco, and rice—the same commodities slave labor produced in the South. Their success in raising these crops, Lundy claimed, would prove to Southern plantation owners that free labor was superior to the slave system. Planters might then emancipate their slaves and hire them as free workers. As his biographer has written, "Economic coercion, Lundy predicted, would work where moral argument had failed." To support this belief, the editor even opened a free-produce store in Baltimore.[53]

In the spring of 1832, Lundy left on a trip to Texas to see for himself if the territory was right for settlement by blacks. This time he did not take the *Genius* with him and, in fact, he traveled under an assumed name for fear that his abolitionist reputation would bring him harm. In Texas, Lundy received encouragement from some territorial officials. However, the officials were more concerned about the growing sentiment in the territory favoring secession from Mexico. When he finally arrived back in Washington and resumed publishing the *Genius,* Lundy continued to tout plans for a Texas colony. In one editorial, he published the many reasons why Texas was the best place for black colonization. These included the "speedy means it will afford the man of color to become wealthy and rise above the degradation that slavery and prejudice has [*sic*] imposed on him" and "FURTHER PROVING to the people of this nation, that here, in America—the land of his birth and his natural home— he may be fitted for freedom and self-government with perfect ease and safety."[54]

Few antislavery leaders endorsed Lundy's plans for a Texas colony. To them Texas was a foreign land, far away from the real fight over the future of slavery. As it grew, the antislavery movement was increasingly engaged in a debate between the "gradualists" on one side and the "immediatists" on the other. Not surprisingly, Lundy's former "apprentice"—as he was to call Garrison—was in the middle of the fight, and the *Liberator* was his chief weapon.

TWO

GROWTH AND CONTROVERSY

To mark what he considered a successful first year of publishing his abolitionist newspaper, William Lloyd Garrison enlarged the size of the *Liberator* at the beginning of 1832 from four columns to five. Although the larger size of the 20-by-25-inch "Royal" sheet would practically double the cost of publishing his controversial weekly, the editor said it was necessary to proclaim the need for immediately ending slavery. "The cause demands a hundred daily presses; larger dimensions must be given to the Liberator," Garrison wrote.[1]

Indeed, over the next several years abolitionists expanded their journalistic efforts with several new publications joining the *Liberator* and the *Genius of Universal Emancipation.* Many of the newspapers were sponsored by the growing number of antislavery societies that sprang up as the movement became more organized. Others were started in various places by free blacks who desperately wanted their own independent editorial voice.

These newspapers supported the creation of the first national abolitionist society, the American Anti-Slavery Society. They also supported the society's efforts to spread the antislavery message through a pamphlet campaign and later a congressional petition drive. The angry reactions that these efforts prompted, including a controversial congressional gag rule, delighted abolitionist editors, who viewed them as signs that they were beginning to have a real impact. When an increasingly defensive South responded by passing laws that prevented the dissemination of abolitionist literature and prohibited the organization of antislavery societies, editors linked these moves to the popular issue of civil liberty.

The widespread outrage directed at him after the bloody Nat Turner rebellion convinced Garrison that abolitionists needed a national organization to carry out the antislavery agenda. That the young editor would be leading the charge testified not only to his confident, headstrong nature but also to the respect he already enjoyed in radical abolitionist circles. Although he had only been publishing his newspaper for a year, the zealous Garrison was already becoming one of the antislavery movement's most dynamic leaders.

In appearance, Garrison was hardly impressive. He was prematurely bald and wore steel-rimmed glasses. He usually dressed in a black suit and black cravat. However, the editor's single-minded devotion to immediately ending slavery, in contrast to the more gradual approach favored by many others, attracted a tight-knit circle of devoted followers. "I remember very distinctly the first time I ever saw Garrison," the popular author Lydia Maria Child wrote years later. "I little thought then that the whole pattern of my life-web would be changed by that introduction . . . He got hold of the strings of my conscience and pulled me into Reforms . . . Old dreams vanished, old associates departed, and all things became new."[2]

In 1831 Garrison had used his newspaper to call for antislavery men and women to organize themselves and "scatter tracts like rain-drops, over the land," spreading the antislavery message. However, other antislavery leaders, concerned that the Turner controversy had done more harm than good for the cause, were wary of creating any organization that bore the stamp of the radical editor. That was not going to stop Garrison, and on November 13, 1831, he gathered a small group that included Samuel May, David L. Child, Samuel Sewall, Arnold Buffman, Oliver Johnson, Joshua Coffin, Moses Thatcher, Ellis Loring Gray, and Isaac Knapp. Garrison spoke passionately about the need to end slavery immediately, but while everyone agreed that should be the group's ultimate goal, many feared putting such radical language in a statement of principles. It took several more meetings—and lots of persuasion by Garrison—before the New England Anti-Slavery Society was finally born at Boston's African Baptist Church on January 1, 1832.[3]

The group declared its support for immediate emancipation, but not in the strong language that the editor wanted. Nonetheless, a buoyant Garrison pronounced that the society would eventually "shake the Nation" into abolishing slavery. He was thrilled that a real organization now would share in the work of agitation. The twelve founders who signed on, Garrison believed, constituted a proper-sized jury "to sit in judgement on the guilt of the country." The society announced that the *Liberator* would be its official publication, although a new publication, the *Abolitionist,* had replaced it in that role by the end of the year. It quickly became clear that Garrison would never let any group—even one he helped start—have any substantial say about what would be printed in his beloved paper.[4]

Although the *Liberator* had many targets in its antislavery campaign, Garrison devoted the most attention to the American Colonization Society. In an early issue of the newspaper, Garrison declared that the society was a "conspiracy against human rights," and he repeated this message time and again. He claimed the society was founded on the pillars of "persecution, falsehood, cowardice [and] infidelity" and that instead of helping the country's blacks, the society actually strengthened slavery. When the New England Anti-Slavery Society began organizing anticolonization rallies throughout the region, he used the *Liberator* to promote them. With financial support from Arthur Tappan, an increasingly important antislavery benefactor, Garrison also published a blistering indictment of the American Colonization Society, his book *Thoughts on African Colonization: or An Impartial Exhibition of the Doctrines, Principles and Purposes of the American Colonization Society, together with the Resolutions, Addresses and Remonstrances of the Free People of Color.* The editor intended to make the 240-page polemic a "textbook" for abolitionist supporters. He admitted that he had once admired the work of the society, writing, "I was then blind, but now I see." Garrison charged that colonization encouraged prejudice and denied blacks the opportunity to raise their status in American society. According to him, God made all nations to dwell upon the earth, and to believe that men and women should be divided into their own communities, each with its own culture, was to misread the divine plan. Garrison argued that the society's work must be stopped or slavery would never be abolished.[5]

Garrison's attack on colonization put him squarely at odds with some antislavery leaders, including his mentor, Benjamin Lundy. The Quaker editor, who continued using his newspaper to work on behalf of colonization, was loath to criticize his friend directly, but he deplored the "severity of personal censure" which Garrison loosed upon anyone who disagreed with his brand of abolitionism. Defending his belief in the wisdom of colonization, Lundy argued that that there should be room under the antislavery tent for a variety of approaches to end the hated institution. "It is not to be expected that this grand reformation can be accomplished by any single system of operation," he wrote in the *Genius*. "The evil of Slavery is one of immense magnitude, and will require the combined efforts of all the wise and virtuous in the nation to eradicate it."[6]

Such thoughts were anathema to Garrison, who saw only one way to end slavery and who increasingly delighted in the notorious reputation he was developing because of his controversial views. As biographer Henry Mayer has pointed out, unlike Lundy, Garrison deliberately chose to make himself an issue in the antislavery fight. "There shall be no neutrals; men shall either like or dislike me," he declared. Garrison wrote about his great delight when strangers realized they were speaking to the hated editor of the *Liberator*. "They had almost imagined me to be in figurine a monster of huge and horrid proportions," he wrote, "but now finding me decently made, *without a single horn,* they take me cordially by the hand, and acknowledge me a 'marvelous proper man.'"[7]

In the spring of 1833 Garrison traveled to England to raise funds for a project that had long been discussed in benevolence circles: a school for blacks that would combine the liberal arts and mechanical trades. The New England Anti-Slavery Society also wanted him to undo the work by a colonization leader who was touring Great Britain and claiming to represent antislavery efforts in the United States. Garrison also hoped to win acceptance as the official representative of American abolitionists. He was more successful with the latter goal, gaining an audience with the aging British abolitionist legend William Wilberforce. He also won kudos from the great Irish orator Daniel O'Connell, who denounced the American Colonization Society and praised Garrison's work.

While Garrison was overseas, a group of New York abolitionists led by Arthur Tappan organized a state antislavery society and launched a new monthly publication, the *Emancipator*. They called a meeting of "The Friends of Immediate Abolition in the United States" for October 2 in Clinton Hall. Garrison, who was arriving back in the United States, was scheduled to speak at the meeting. Opponents of the antislavery movement, including some in the press, used his appearance to whip thousands of New Yorkers into a frenzy. Tappan and his friends learned of the mob and moved their meeting to the Chatham Street Chapel. When the crowd learned what had happened, they descended on the chapel. However, by that time the abolitionists had hastily concluded their business and fled out a back door. Determined to enjoy their triumph, the crowd held a mock abolitionist meeting presided over by a terrified black man whom they forced to pose as "Arthur Tappan." The meeting included many ribald speeches and racially offensive resolutions.[8]

Garrison never made it to the antislavery meeting. He walked off the ship from England only to find himself overrun by the angry crowd headed for Clinton Hall. The editor tried to get to the Chatham Street Chapel but never made it. Unrecognized, he stood at the edge of the mob as it banged on the gates of the chapel trying to get in. He stayed with friends that night and then immediately traveled back home to Boston. Once back at his editor's desk, Garrison described his mixed feelings of "pity and contempt" for the mob. Not surprisingly, he boasted that the "triumphant success" of his trip to England was behind the protest. "Had I failed to vanquish the agent of the American Colonization Society, or to open the eyes of the British philanthropists to its naked deformity, there would have been no excitement upon my return," he wrote in the *Liberator.* Garrison declared that he was "ready to brave any danger, even unto death" for the abolitionist cause.[9]

By 1833 local antislavery societies were scattered across many states of the North. Although the New England Anti-Slavery Society and other state umbrella groups had been successful in encouraging the growth of grassroots societies, most were small and had little influence beyond their immediate areas. Abolitionist leaders decided the time had come for a national antislavery society, especially while the action of the New York mob was fresh in people's minds.

Leaders of the New York group sent out a letter inviting all friends of antislavery to meet in Philadelphia on December 4 to "take counsel together and *go forward*" with a national organization. Sixty-three delegates from ten states attended the convention. In addition to the New Yorkers, the delegates included a sizable group from New England, Quakers from Pennsylvania, and evangelicals from Ohio, as well as Presbyterian, Congregational, and Unitarian ministers. The group also included four women and three blacks. City leaders, who feared the outbreak of violence, insisted that the three-day meeting be held in the daytime hours. Even so, delegates were often taunted with racist epithets as they made their way to Adelphia Hall, a small building next to the oldest black church in the city.

On the first day of the convention, a committee was appointed to draft a constitution. The committee promptly assigned three members—Garrison, Samuel May, and John Greenleaf Whittier—to write a Declaration of Sentiments, which would serve as a platform for the society. The declaration began with a pointed reference to the signing of the Declaration of Independence in Philadelphia fifty-seven years earlier. The founding fathers had "waged war against their oppressors" in order to be free, it noted, yet their grievances against Britain "were trifling in comparison with those of the slaves." The document demanded the immediate, unconditional emancipation of slaves. It said that for citizens who enjoyed the blessings of liberty, toleration of slavery amounted to a personal sin "unequalled by any other on the face of the earth." Although a handful of delegates opposed some of the language in the declaration, it was largely accepted as written. Before the convention ended, the delegates solemnly walked up to the platform one by one and affixed their signatures to the declaration of the new American Anti-Slavery Society.[10]

For the great majority of Americans, the idea of immediate emancipation was sheer fanaticism. And, indeed, what the immediatists were proposing was radical beyond anything seen in the nation's history in its social, political, and economic implications. Emancipation not only would overturn Southern society, but it would also mean a new era in capitalist America, as free blacks would compete with whites for jobs. None of this mattered to the organizers of the society, who saw themselves, in the words of James Brewer Stewart, as "the prophets of a new age." Abolitionists saw themselves in a "righteous war to redeem a fallen nation." As one lecturer wrote in 1835, "Never were men called on to die in a holier cause."[11]

Society members pledged to organize antislavery societies in every town and city across the country. To spread its message the society would sponsor traveling antislavery agents and use the press, publishing tracts and newspapers. Its methods were the same that had been used by evangelical religious denominations for decades. And like the revivalists, abolitionist leaders believed that slaveholders and others who supported the institution—either outwardly or through indifference—could be convinced of the evils of slavery. They called this approach "moral suasion."

Talented writers such as Whittier, Child, Angelina Grimké, and Amos A. Phelps had been publishing antislavery literature for years. But in 1835 the American Anti-Slavery Society embarked on a crusade of moral suasion with an aggressive program designed to "sow the good seed of abolition thoroughly over the whole country." The campaign took various forms, but the centerpiece was a pamphlet campaign designed to make the public aware of the society's antislavery work. With a budget of $30,000—much of it donated by philanthropists such as Tappan—the society flooded the North and South with abolitionist literature. The targets were ministers, newspaper editors, elected officials, and other prominent citizens—approximately 20,000 in the South alone. These molders of local opinion, the society's leaders believed, would learn about the moral depravity of slavery from the free literature and help turn the public against it.[12]

Like so much of the antislavery movement, the pamphlet campaign was patterned after the work of evangelical denominations that had been mass-mailing religious literature for decades. Thanks to new printing technology—including stereotyped plates, paper-cutting machines, and steam presses—mass printing could be done faster and cheaper than ever before. Pioneering "penny papers" in New York, such as the *Sun,* were using new steam-powered Hoe cylinder presses to print 1,000 papers an hour, as opposed to the 200 turned out with the old hand presses. Near the American Anti-Slavery Society office on Nassau Street in New York, the publishing giant Harper Brothers had installed power presses that were turning out a million books a year.[13]

The materials produced by the abolitionists were often referred to as pamphlets, but they were more like modern-day newspapers or magazines. They included a folio paper, *Human Rights;* a magazine, the *Anti-Slavery Record;* a juvenile tract, the *Slave's Friend;* and the society's newspaper, the *Emancipator,* which was changed from a weekly to a monthly. These publications carried a wide variety of materials: antislavery fiction and poems, accounts of fugitive slaves, reports of slave kidnappings, criticism of colonization plans, and stories of free blacks. Some of the material in the pamphlets was unquestionably inflammatory. One cover of the *Anti-Slavery Record* showed a white planter holding a black baby by the wrist and whipping the child's weeping mother with the other hand. Another showed a slave mother using an axe to kill her twin infants who were to be sold and taken away from her. The language in the pamphlets was likewise inflammatory. The *Anti-Slavery Record* declared that slaveholders should be on a "list of felons" who deserved to be excluded from "the society of honest men as the pickpocket, the counterfeiter, or highway robber." By the summer of 1836 more than a million pieces of literature had been distributed.[14]

The publication *Human Rights* predicted that some Southerners would "rave and scold and threaten" upon reading the literature—and it was right. The arrival of the publications caused hysteria in many communities, both in the South and North. Elected officials, merchants, clergymen, and editors decried

what they saw as a dangerous conspiracy by fanatical abolitionists that would turn the country on its head. Citizen meetings
demanded a stop to the publications, and groups sometimes took
matters into their own hands.[15]

After hearing rumors that abolitionist literature had arrived
in the mail, angry residents of Charleston, South Carolina,
broke into the post office, hauled away the mailbags, and burned
them in the street. The mob then hung effigies of Garrison and
Tappan. The next month a citywide meeting expressed "abhorrence and detestation" at the attempt "to deluge our State with
Incendiary publications." A committee of twenty-one members
was appointed to work with the postmaster to inspect the mail
and burn any objectionable materials. Additionally, the city
council offered a reward of $1,000 for the apprehension of any
person bringing any such materials into the city or distributing
them. The council also declared that any person who received
the literature or communicated with antislavery societies was,
in its words, "an enemy of the state."[16]

At the same time, the postmaster of Charleston wrote
Postmaster General Amos Kendall asking what he should do
with future shipments of antislavery publications. Kendall
replied that although the publications were within the letter of
the postal laws, they were clearly inflammatory, and that justified not distributing them. "I cannot sanction, and will not
condemn, the steps you have taken," he wrote. "We owe an
obligation to the laws, but a higher one to the communities in
which we live." Any postmaster who stopped distribution of
"inflammatory papers," Kendall wrote, "would stand justified
before country and all mankind."[17]

Kendall's position was supported by many communities in
both the South and the North. A Virginia community passed a

resolution to "sustain all postmasters in detaining and publicly destroying all abolition papers." Similar resolutions supporting the destruction of abolitionist literature were passed by communities in Virginia, Alabama, and Mississippi, as well as Pennsylvania, New Jersey, Massachusetts, and New Hampshire. A meeting in Portland, Maine, declared that sending abolitionist materials through the mail was "an alarming perversion and abuse of this invaluable medium of communication." A meeting in Richmond, Virginia, appointed a vigilance committee to keep watch over post offices, hotels, and ships for abolitionist materials. For his part, President Andrew Jackson publicly criticized the campaign and voiced support for the measures banning abolitionist literature. In his annual message to Congress in December 1835, Jackson called on lawmakers to pass a federal law prohibiting the circulation of "incendiary publications intended to instigate the slaves to insurrection."[18]

Eventually every Southern state, with the exception of Kentucky, passed laws preventing the dissemination of abolitionist literature and prohibiting the organization of antislavery societies within its borders. A Virginia code, for example, punished by fines up to $500 and imprisonment for up to a year any person who "by speaking or writing maintains that owners have no right of property in slaves." Louisiana set penalties of hard labor or even death for conversation "having a tendency to promote discontent among free colored people, or insubordination among slaves." Southern legislatures also demanded that Northern states take action against the publishers of abolitionist materials. They received a sympathetic response from several state legislatures which introduced bills to regulate antislavery publications, although none passed. Only Pennsylvania and Ohio passed resolutions that expressed the unconstitutionality of such controls.[19]

Vigilance committees in Southern communities ensured that the laws were enforced through their own brand of "justice." They interrogated travelers and inspected bags to ensure that no abolitionist materials were distributed. The most widely publicized case of vigilance committee justice took place in Nashville, Tennessee, when Amos Dresser, a student from Lane Theological Seminary, was caught with a parcel of Bibles wrapped in a copy of the *Emancipator*. He was found guilty by the committee of belonging to an abolitionist society, of possessing antislavery literature, and of distributing the material. He was publicly whipped, his belongings were confiscated, and he was ordered to leave town.

Abolitionist newspapers reprinted parts or all of the pamphlets and took every opportunity to extol the virtues of the campaign. They decried the measures blocking abolitionist literature as clear violations of First Amendment freedoms. The *Liberator* regularly published the measures in its "Refuge of Oppression" column, usually following them with stinging commentary. A public meeting in Barnwell, South Carolina, passed resolutions expressing opposition to the distribution of abolitionist material and declaring that the authors of the material were not entitled to legal protection. "If such be the general sentiments of this state . . ." the *Liberator* declared, "then their state is lost beyond recovery, to any redeeming good." Editors also cited cases of their own publications being destroyed or not disseminated by postal employees. James G. Birney, editor of the *Philanthropist,* assailed a Kentucky postmaster who threw out copies of the abolitionist newspaper. The papers were not addressed to the postmaster's office, Birney complained, but only passed through on their way up the Ohio River to subscribers in Pittsburgh. "We are charged with full postage," an angry Birney wrote, "yet we are denied, because our observations do not coincide with those of some of its officers, a just return of its benefits."[20]

Abolitionist editors made sure their readers understood the extent of vigilance committee activity, pointing out when the groups were formed in Southern communities and describing their actions. One newspaper told the story of a British sea captain who was beaten by a mob in Florida for his antislavery views. Another paper described how the son of a Quaker abolitionist narrowly escaped a mob after a vigilance committee found an antislavery pamphlet in his baggage. Still another described the case of a Presbyterian minister who was manhandled by a committee for reading a letter on slavery in church.

Editors also publicized the rewards offered by vigilance committees for the apprehension of offenders, adding their own stinging commentary about the absurdity of such measures in a country dedicated to liberty. A committee in Savannah, Georgia, offered $10,000 for Amos A. Phelps, and a committee in Mount Meigs, Alabama, posted a reward of $50,000 for Arthur Tappan. One Louisiana committee had a standing offer of $500 for "any abolitionists whatsoever." Abolitionist editors also reprinted articles from Southern newspapers justifying the existence of vigilance committees. One paper quoted from a South Carolina committee which concluded that "where the laws of the land are insufficient to meet the emergency . . . we *are deliberately and advisedly determined* that the *guilty shall not escape.*"[21]

Among the publications expressing outrage were a host of new abolitionist newspapers. The New Hampshire Anti-Slavery Society founded the *Herald of Freedom* in 1835 with Nathaniel Rogers as editor. William Goodell, the former editor of the *Emancipator*, moved to Utica to start the *Friend of Man,* a new publication sponsored by the New York State Anti-Slavery Society.

Meanwhile, the *Emancipator* was switched back to a weekly in 1836, and Joshua Leavitt became its editor the following year. A graduate of Yale, Leavitt had practiced law but was swept up in the evangelical revivalism of the 1820s. He returned to school to study theology and served as a Congregationalist minister. He then was named editor of the *Evangelist,* a religious publication based in New York. Leavitt also became an abolitionist and was one of the leaders of the New York City Anti-Slavery Society when he was tapped to be editor of the *Emancipator,* a publication that had suffered from undistinguished leadership. The energetic and outspoken Leavitt put his own stamp on the newspaper, one that would increasingly put him at odds with Garrison.[22]

Virtually all abolitionist publications by this point shared a common format. Most were four pages and published weekly. The first page of each issue generally featured a long lead article, often an antislavery speech or minutes of an abolitionist meeting. The second and third pages carried editorials, letters to the editor, stories about slavery and the slave trade, and notices of upcoming events. The fourth page often consisted of poetry or prose, generally on an antislavery subject. A good deal of the content was local, but to keep readers apprised of news from across the country, editors exchanged their papers free of charge with one another. A good deal of the content was local, but to keep readers apprised of news from across the country, editors took full advantage of the exchange system, trading papers free of charge with their fellow antislavery editors.

Also joining the ranks of new publications were several new black-owned newspapers. Since the founding of *Freedom's Journal* and *Rights of All,* newspapers published by free blacks had struggled mightily to gain any kind of foothold. A few black papers were started in the 1830s, but most lasted less than a year. Financial problems plagued all black-owned newspapers, as they did for most antislavery publications. But the problems were more acute for black papers because they were aimed primarily at the small population of free blacks who could afford a newspaper. Without other financial support, there was simply an insufficient number of paying subscribers to keep most black papers in business.[23]

One of the more successful black-owned publications was the *Colored American,* founded by Phillip Bell in 1837. Bell had no journalism experience, but he was one of New York's leading black businessmen. Samuel Cornish, one of the founders of *Freedom's Journal,* had stayed in New York to establish an antislavery society in the city, and he soon joined the *Colored American.* Cornish said the title of the newspaper was chosen because blacks were "emphatically" Americans and nothing else. As for the term *Colored,* he said, it was the name considered most acceptable by most of the race. "We are written about, preached to, and prayed for, as *Negroes, Africans,* and *blacks,* all of which have been stereotyped, as terms of the reproach, and on that account, if no other, are unacceptable," Cornish wrote.[24]

The conservative Cornish emphasized time and again in the pages of the newspaper that free blacks had a responsibility to lead upstanding lives. "Each one for himself, must commence the improvement of his condition," he wrote. "It is not in mass, but in individual effort and character, that we are to move onward, to higher elevation." Failure to do so, he argued, would provide their enemies with arguments with which to oppose ending slavery. "On *our* conduct, in great measure, *their* salvation depends," the editor wrote. "Let us show that we are worthy to be freemen; it will be the strongest appeal to the judgement and conscience of the slave-holder and his abettors that can be furnished and it will be a sure means of our elevation in society, and to the possession of all our rights, as men and citizens."[25]

The best hope of the slaves was the new American Anti-Slavery Society, Cornish argued. All other groups, including the church, had compromised with "the sin of prejudice." "We can have no confidence in nor expect any thing from her," he wrote. At the same time, the *Colored American* was a sharp critic of colonization. Cornish suggested that blacks "would rather die a thousand deaths" than willingly leave the United States for another home. "No country presents so many advantages as the land of our birth," he wrote. "We will stay and seek the purification of the whole lump."[26]

But more than anything, Cornish promoted the Protestant work ethic, emphasizing self-help and personal responsibility for blacks. As an educated member of the black middle class in New York, he was dismayed by what he too often saw among the city's black residents. He challenged blacks to throw off the "useless, vulgar, and sinful habits and practices" of bondage. Failure to do so would provide their enemies with arguments with which to "oppose the emancipation of the slave, and to hinder the education of the free." Blacks should ask for no special treatment and no favors because of the color of their skin. "We would have our friends and brethren know," Cornish wrote, "unless our moral and intellectual attainments *be measured by the same rule, and brought to the same standard* by which our white brethren are tried and estimated, we cannot occupy the same place in society, nor be held in the same repute."

The *Colored American* also emphasized the importance of education. "We must avail ourselves of all the means of public and private education," Cornish wrote, "husband our resources, and expend a fair proportion of them in the establishment of libraries, reading rooms, useful lectures and all the machinery of useful, *practical knowledge and refinement.*" Cornish pointed to the trials he had endured in being a largely uneducated black man. The editor also preached the importance of civic virtue. "If we would have our children accomplished and efficient citizens of our beloved country," he wrote, "we must set the example, by identifying ourselves and them, with all the interests of the government."[27]

The *Colored American's* slogan was "Righteousness Exalteth a Nation," and Cornish praised the work of abolitionists for having led a moral revolution in the country. "They have created a conscience *before God and the world,*" he wrote, "which pervades all the length and breadth of our country, and which can never be appeased whilst there is a slave in the land." But the editor criticized abolitionists for demanding less from blacks because of their presumed inferiority. The *Colored American* also warned free blacks that as long as they let white abolitionists act for them, "they will outwardly treat us as men, while in their hearts they still hold us slaves."[28]

Although the pamphlet campaign caused plenty of controversy, it produced few converts to the antislavery cause. The pamphlets were expensive to produce, and because of distribution problems, no one could be sure they were even widely read by the people most targeted. Some abolitionist leaders privately considered the campaign a costly failure.[29]

Antislavery groups soon turned to another device—congressional petitions—and once again newspapers widely supported the drive. The practice of sending antislavery petitions to

Congress went back to the 1790s, when Pennsylvania Quakers and the Pennsylvania Society for the Abolition of Slavery used them to peacefully protest their opposition to the slave trade. Each subsequent session of Congress received various petitions requesting the abolishment of the slave trade, an end to slavery in the District of Columbia, and gradual emancipation of all slaves, among other issues. The petitions were usually received without comment and referred to a congressional committee where they soon died for lack of action.[30]

But starting in the early 1830s petitions increasingly came from antislavery societies, and their calls for immediate emancipation were far more forceful. Southern leaders in Congress, already on the defensive about slavery, viewed the petitions as a threat, and they decided to put a stop to them. In 1836 a congressional committee led by Henry L. Pinckney of South Carolina recommended that "all petitions, memorials, resolutions, propositions, or papers relating in any way or to any extent whatever to the subject of slavery or the abolition of slavery shall, without being printed or referred, be laid upon the table, and that no further action whatever be taken thereon." Despite the opposition of some Northern congressmen, who called the bill a direct violation of constitutional freedoms, the Pinckney "gag rule" passed.[31]

This latest attempt to block antislavery action enraged abolitionists, and they decided to embarrass Congress by flooding its members with petitions. The American Anti-Slavery Society mobilized local antislavery groups across the North to send petitions to congressmen, believing a blitz of petitions would force a discussion of slavery in Congress, as well as unify abolitionists across the country around a common issue. "Every name signed to a petition," said Henry B. Stanton, "is a nail driven into the coffin of slavery." During the first eighteen months of the campaign, some 300,000 petitions landed on the desks of congressmen, both North and South. They included petitions supporting the abolition of slavery in the District of Columbia, petitions forbidding slavery in the territories, petitions against the interstate slave trade, and petitions calling for repeal of the gag rule.[32]

Abolitionist editors did everything they could to support the petition drive. They printed detailed instructions for preparing, signing, and mailing petitions. They reprinted various petitions to be copied and used. And in angry editorials they blistered Congress for a lack of action. "It is becoming more and more evident," the *Liberator* proclaimed, "that northern liberty is the mere foot-ball of southern tyrants; that any alliance with these monsters is incompatible with our rights and safety as a people." After the House of Representatives effectively buried thousands of petitions by referring them to a committee, the *Emancipator* implored its readers: "If Congress can bury 10,000 names this year, let them have 20,000 next year, and 40,000 the next, and so on till at length some member is obliged, at least, to pronounce a decent funeral oration." Editors also repeatedly quoted Southern leaders who warned against threats such as the petitions to end slavery in the District of Columbia. The governor of South Carolina, for example, warned: "When this crisis shall arrive, those who now claim for Congress the constitutional power to emancipate the slaves in the District of Columbia, will as boldly claim the same power in regard to the states—their whole course demonstrates that this is the consummation at which they are aiming."[33]

The gag rule provoked bitter debate in Congress for years. Led by former President John Quincy Adams, who had been elected to the House of Representatives, some congressmen fought to repeal the gag rule each year, citing the threat to civil liberties. They argued that the right of petition meant the right to have petitions considered. If it did not, then what use was the privilege, they asked? However, they were always defeated by Southern members and their supporters, who were determined to protect slavery from all attacks. The Southern representatives maintained that slavery was a state issue and, since Congress had no power over the institution, petitions requesting Congress to legislate against it should not be considered. Moreover, abolishing slavery was a threat to Southern property and was therefore unconstitutional. "We can never be more united or better prepared for the struggle," said South Carolina's John C. Calhoun, "and I, for one, would rather meet the danger now, than turn it over to those who are to come after us." At one point, a group of Southern congressmen even introduced a censure resolution against Adams, accusing him of contempt and treason, among other crimes. It did not pass. But a new gag rule was approved at the beginning of each session of Congress until 1845.[34]

Abolitionist newspapers did their best to keep the issue before readers, reprinting the congressional debates, praising opponents of the gag rule, and ridiculing them for some of their actions, such as the censure resolution against Adams. They applauded the former president and his fellow congressmen for standing up to the "Northern dough-faces" who cowered at the threats by the South. They also pointed out something that was becoming evident to many people, including opponents of the antislavery movement—that the gag rule controversy allowed abolitionists to link their cause with the popular issue of civil liberty. And that was attracting new adherents to the antislavery cause. "If the right of petition be abridged or annuled [*sic*], we shall have made the first step toward despotism," the *Liberator* quoted a Philadelphia newspaper as declaring. And a New York newspaper editorialized: "We have ever thought that the actual slavery of one portion of the people must eventually lead to the virtual slavery of the other, and both ancient history and modern example seem to confirm the opinion." One publication quoted John Botts of Virginia, who said that the argument over petitions "made more abolitionists in one year, by identifying the right of petition with the question of slavery, than the abolitionists would have made for themselves in twenty-five years."[35]

During the controversy over the congressional petition drive, Garrison reprinted the popular story from *Pilgrim's Progress* of Christian and Faithful's trip to the Celestial City on the front page of the *Liberator*. To Garrison, John Bunyan's allegorical tale of the pilgrims, who spurned the worldly vices of Vanity Fair in a search for the truth but were beaten and jailed for disturbing the peace, was just like "the case of modern abolitionists in this country." Like Bunyan's brave travelers, one of whom was burned at the stake because he declared his allegiance to God instead of popular customs, Garrison proclaimed that the country's antislavery men and women would have to endure great hostility in order for people to see the wickedness and inhumanity of the slave system. Little did the *Liberator*'s editor know at the time just how accurate his prediction about violence would turn out to be—or that he and other abolitionist editors would be so swept up in it.[36]

THREE

THE PRESS UNDER ATTACK

The handbill distributed around Cincinnati in July 1836 could not have been any more clear. Warning "Abolitionist[s]? Beware," it defended the recent attack on the city's new abolitionist newspaper, the *Philanthropist*. On July 12, a group of citizens had broken into the office of the paper's printer, destroying the next issue and wrecking printing equipment. Now the handbill asked for the public's support "to eradicate an evil which every citizen feels is undermining his business and property." It also warned that if the *Philanthropist* resumed publishing, it would "be viewed as an act of defiance to an already outraged community, and on their heads will be the results which will follow."[1]

To no one's surprise, *Philanthropist* publisher James G. Birney ignored the message. A former slaveholder who had become a devoted abolitionist, Birney argued that publishing the weekly was a test of personal freedom in the North. "Must we trample on the liberty of white men here because they have trampled on the liberty of black men in the South?" he asked in an editorial. "Must we forge chains for the *mind* here, because they have forged them for the *body* there? Must we extinguish the right to

speak, the right to *print* in the North, that we may be in unison
with the South? No, never." Angry residents of Cincinnati
returned two weeks later. After breaking into the printing office
for a second time, they tied a rope around the press, dragged it
down the street, and pushed it into the Ohio River.[2]

The destruction of the *Philanthropist*'s press was just one in a
series of riotous incidents against abolitionist editors and anti-
slavery supporters in general during the mid-1830s. Violence
directed at the press occurred right up to the beginning of the
Civil War, but it reached its height when, in the space of three
years, not only was the *Philanthropist* wrecked, but a Boston
crowd attacked William Lloyd Garrison, editor Elijah Lovejoy
was killed by an Illinois mob trying to wreck his abolitionist
weekly, and Benjamin Lundy saw his belongings destroyed in
a fire set by rioting Philadelphians. Antislavery editors seized
upon the repressive tactics directed against them as proof of the
spreading evil of slavery. They claimed they were loyal Americans
who were only interested in improving the lives of blacks. They
also argued that the actions of the mobs threatened fundamental
democratic principles, including freedom of the press.[3]

Generally speaking, mob violence directed at abolitionists
began with the protests that disrupted the New York antislavery
meeting in October 1833. The abolitionist goal of immediate
emancipation raised long-standing fears of many Americans
about racial assimilation. As travelers to the United States had
noted for years, fear and hatred of blacks flourished in both the
South and North. Although all the Northern states had outlawed
slavery by 1825, laws still discriminated against blacks in myriad
ways. In most places, free blacks were prevented from voting
and serving on juries. They were barred from many restau-

rants, hotels, and theaters. They were also segregated in schools, churches, hospitals, and even cemeteries. As Leon Litwack has written, "In virtually every phase of existence [blacks] found themselves systematically separated from whites."[4]

At the same time, violent protests were becoming an accepted way of dealing with the ethnic, social, political, and religious strains facing a growing and increasingly diverse young country. The *Liberator* quoted an Ohio correspondent who wrote in 1836: "When a body of men with such feelings and principles begins to distract the nation with their mad schemes, it is high time for a community to notice. I am no advocate of Lynch law, but I must say that if Lynch law is to be practiced, I know of no fitter subjects for its operation than such fanatics." To a certain extent, the ethos of Jacksonian society encouraged citizens to participate enthusiastically in shaping public life, even if that meant resorting to violence. President Andrew Jackson himself was a model for this, as he abolished banks and defied the courts. Many antebellum Americans came to believe, as one historian of the era has written, "that man standing above the law was not to be a threat to society, but its fulfillment."[5]

The opponents of abolitionism who resorted to violence claimed they were simply protecting the established order against dangerous and radical outsiders who were bent on disrupting the community. Generally led by a core group of respectable citizens, including lawyers, bankers, clergymen, and politicians, these opponents often held formal meetings, elected a group of executive officers, and passed resolutions before doing their "duty." Many identified themselves with the Sons of Liberty, the Minutemen, and other patriot groups who had fought against the tyranny of British rule. One Philadelphia mob even went so far as to emulate the Boston Tea Party. The protesters seized abolitionist pamphlets, hauled them out into the Delaware River, and proudly dumped them overboard.

The mob activities clearly violated federal and state laws guaranteeing freedom of speech and expression. However, to some extent the mobs also were protected by the eighteenth-century legal view that communities should have some control over ideas disseminated in their midst in order to protect the citizenry. This common-law doctrine for regulating community activities placed majority interests over individual rights. At the same time, nineteenth-century law left many regulatory responsibilities to local authorities. All this meant that, when confronted with an antislavery publisher expressing unpopular views in a community, protesters could draw on legal principles to stop him from publishing—even if it meant resorting to violence.[6]

The mobs were often encouraged by political leaders, as well as the mainstream press. Governor J. H. Hammond of South Carolina told his state legislature that a group of citizens who suppressed abolitionist activity was "no more a mob than a rally of shepherds to chase a wolf out of their pastures." The *Boston Courier and Enquirer* believed that if abolitionists "openly and publicly promulgate doctrines which outrage public feeling, they have no right to demand protection from the people they insult." In issuing a thinly veiled call for action against an abolitionist meeting, the *New York Courier and Enquirer* asked, "Are we tamely to look on, and see this most dangerous species of fanaticism extending itself through society?" The proper course of action, the paper declared, was to extinguish "this many-headed Hydra in the bud." Such prompt action would expose "the folly, madness, and mischief of these bold and dangerous men."[7]

Once the mob violence began, few places seemed to escape it. A Methodist minister who supported the abolitionists was attacked on the streets of Worcester, Massachusetts. When an antislavery lecturer attempted to speak in a Granville, Ohio, schoolhouse, protesters drove him off and burned the school. Residents of New Canaan, New Hampshire, hitched a yoke of oxen to a multiracial school and dragged it to a nearby swamp. In several instances the violence spread throughout a community. Angry whites in Philadelphia destroyed more than forty homes owned by free blacks. In the summer of 1835, a mob in New York City wrecked the homes of leading abolitionists and then destroyed black schools, homes, and businesses. The violence prompted Lydia Maria Child to write: "I have not ventured into the city . . . so great is the excitement here . . .'Tis like the times of the French Revolution, when no man dared to trust his neighbors."[8]

Abolitionist editors seized every opportunity to report various examples of mob violence as proof of the spreading sin of slavery. "And what has brought our country to the verge of ruin . . . THE ACCURSED SYSTEM OF SLAVERY!" Garrison thundered in the *Liberator*. "To sustain that system, there is a general willingness to destroy LIBERTY of SPEECH and of the PRESS, and to mob or murder all who oppose it." Editors also implored supporters not to give in to the intimidating tactics of their opponents. One editorial reminded speakers: "Every abolition lecture they break up is a ruinous victory to the cause of slavery." It advised speakers to not provoke mobs and do everything to avoid them. If a mob tried to break up a meeting, continue and hope the protesters would eventually tire. "Be persecuted if you must," the editorial implored.[9]

Certainly, the abolitionist press gave plenty of attention to the makeup of the mobs. One publication said they were drawn first from "the aristocracy of wealth," who saw the abolitionist movement as a threat to their economic interest; second, from those who were "unwilling that the negroes should be turned loose to remain among us in the full enjoyment of equal rights"; and third, from the lower ranks of society, "drunken and deceived mobocrats whose arguments consist of vulgar black-guardism, brickbats, and rotten eggs." Abolitionist editors also pointed out with delight that mainstream newspapers sometimes encouraged the mob violence in the North. One antislavery publication quoted the *Day Book,* New York's most violently anti-abolitionist paper, in saying it hoped for the day when "an Abolitionist will be lynched as readily in New York and Boston as in Charleston or New Orleans."[10]

Antislavery leaders believed that the mob violence directed at abolitionists only drew attention to the cause—and they exulted. "The cause *is* progressing," John Greenleaf Whittier wrote. "I want no better evidence of it than the rabid violence of our enemies." In editorial after editorial, antislavery publications constantly hammered home the theme that mob attacks were a suppression of free speech and a clear threat to constitutional liberties. "When we first unfurled the banner of the Liberator," Garrison wrote, "we did not anticipate that, in order to protect southern slavery, the free states would voluntarily trample under foot all order, law and government, or brand the advocates of universal liberty as incendiaries."[11]

Not surprisingly, a target of mob violence was the hated Garrison. In the summer of 1835, New England was in a fury over the visit of the English abolitionist lecturer George Thompson. Thompson had started his tour in Maine and New Hampshire, where protesters repeatedly tried to break up his speaking engagements. At a meeting in Concord, New Hampshire, angry audience members threw eggs and stones at the abolitionist. A crowd at another meeting mistook Whittier for Thompson and pelted him with various items. Thompson was denounced as an agent of "foreign interference" and a "stirrer-up of strife." By the time he was scheduled to visit Boston, mobs were attacking residents of what was known as "Nigger Hill," looting their homes and driving them off the streets. Several of the city's daily newspapers fanned the opposition to Thompson, calling him an agent of the enemies of "republican institutions."[12]

Never one to avoid a fight, Garrison responded to the violence in his hometown with characteristic fury. He lashed out at what he called the "utter degeneracy" of Boston. He particularly singled out "the high and educated classes" for their sinful prejudice against blacks. Although they did not constitute the largest part of the mob, Garrison claimed they were "the most to blame." Citizens responded by erecting a gallows in front of the editor's home while he was away. The chilling structure was draped with seaweed from the nearby tidal flats, and a note was attached to it from "Judge Lynch." Before Thompson's speech to the Boston Female Anti-Slavery Society, 500 handbills were distributed around the city urging "friends of the Union" to a rally "to snake out . . . that infamous foreign scoundrel Thompson." The handbills offered a $100 reward to "the individual who shall first lay violent hands on Thompson, so that he may be brought to the tar-kettle before dark."[13]

An angry crowd packed the meeting hall on October 21 for the lecture. When Thompson did not appear, the mob shouted for Garrison, crying "Lynch him" and "Turn him a right nigger color with tar." When it became clear that a riot would ensue if

Garrison spoke, leaders of the society urged him to leave. The editor slipped out a back window of the hall but was spotted hiding in a nearby carpenter's shop. The crowd tied a rope around Garrison and marched him down the street, presumably to be tarred and feathered. Before they could get far, police responded and beat off the attackers, but not before they had ripped Garrison's clothes off his back. He was put in a city jail for safekeeping and spent the evening in a suit of borrowed clothes. While in the cell, Garrison inscribed a message on the wall: "William Lloyd Garrison was put into this cell on Wednesday afternoon, October 21, 1835, to save him from the violence of a 'respectable and influential' mob, who sought to destroy him for preaching the abominable and dangerous doctrine that 'all men are created equal' and that all oppression is odious in the sight of God." Boston authorities released Garrison the next day on the condition that he leave the city for a time.[14]

The *Liberator*'s office was spared during the violence, and its press soon turned out accounts of the affair, including one from Garrison himself. "Give me brickbats in the cause of God, to wedges of gold in the cause of sin," the editor declared. Boston newspapers responded by blaming abolitionists for the crowd's action. The *Atlas* said Garrison had been properly jailed as "a public agitator," and the *Daily Advertiser* declared that the affair was "not so much as a *riot* as the *prevention of a riot*." The *Transcript* expressed satisfaction that the mob had been a respectable group and was not made up of the ruffians that comprised gangs in other cities. But it was the *Commercial Gazette* that coined the term that abolitionists would endlessly repeat sarcastically in describing mobs. The newspaper said the assemblage was simply "a meeting of *gentlemen of property and standing*" who wanted to preserve the peace.[15]

Not surprisingly, Garrison seemed to enjoy the martyrdom. Hyperbole filled his later description of the "reign of terror" that had led to his attack. "A cloud of infamy—a thunder-cloud of heaven's vengeance—a cloud of darkness and terror, covers the nation like a mighty pall," he thundered. "Rebellious, ungrateful and blood-thirsty land! how are thou fallen even to the lowest depths of degradation and sin." He also lashed out at the mainstream press in Boston. Garrison noted that before the protests erupted in 1835, only one newspaper in the city did not encourage mob action.[16]

Certainly, Cincinnati's newspapers helped to whip up opposition to the *Philanthropist* when James G. Birney announced his plans to start an abolitionist publication in the city. A former slaveholder in Alabama, Birney was already well known when he moved to the "Queen City of the West" in 1835. Born into an aristocratic Kentucky family that owned slaves, Birney graduated from Princeton and then studied law in Philadelphia. He returned to Kentucky and soon was elected to the state legislature. At the urging of a fellow member of the legislature, Birney decided to move his family to the new territory of Alabama where he could become a lawyer and planter, the customary path of many Southern gentlemen. However, Birney was soon swept up in the revival spirit that was spreading across the country, and he became a devoted Presbyterian.[17]

Inspired with the Christian duty to help his fellow man, Birney became concerned about the plight of slaves. He initially supported colonization and became a leader of a new colonization society in the state. However, Birney became disenchanted with colonization because he believed it did not address the problem of slavery as an institution. Abolitionist leaders recognized that as an aristocratic Southerner who had once owned slaves, Birney could be a powerful symbol and spokesman in the antislavery fight. With the encouragement of Arthur Tappan, Birney decided to start an abolitionist newspaper. He originally planned to publish the paper in his hometown of Danville, Kentucky, but decided against it after being roundly criticized. Abolitionist leaders suggested Cincinnati as a promising location, and Birney agreed.

Slavery had never been permitted in Cincinnati, but the institution enjoyed considerable support in the city. Only the Ohio River separated Cincinnati from the South, and slave owners traveled to the city regularly, often bringing their slaves with them. The city's booming economy was fueled in part by trade with the South. Cincinnati was also the home of an increasing number of free blacks, many of whom were articulate and outspoken. Blacks in the city celebrated the anniversary of American independence on the fifth of July instead of the fourth.[18]

Soon after Birney arrived, a group of prominent citizens, including the mayor, the city marshal, and the editor of the *Cincinnati Gazette,* visited the editor and warned him that he could expect violence if he published "incendiary" materials. Birney thanked the men for their concern but said he would not surrender his civil rights to "whatever might be the madness and folly of those who might choose to assail them." With the help of his sons, he armed his home with muskets and shotguns and began making plans to publish his newspaper.

The first issue of the *Philanthropist* appeared on January 1, 1836, bearing the biblical motto, "We are verily guilty concerning our brother * * * therefore, is this distress come upon us." Recognizing that he was publishing in a city with many Southern sympathizers, Birney carefully avoided the provocative language of newspapers like the *Liberator* and invited discussion of the slavery issue from both sides. The first issue carried a lengthy vindication of abolitionists, in which Birney answered the criticism of antislavery men. Birney said antislavery societies were peaceful organizations and had not incited the slaves to rebellion. He argued that slaveholders violated freedom of speech and the press with their laws prohibiting the distribution of abolitionist materials. He also invited them to present their side of the issue in the *Philanthropist*. To demonstrate his sincerity, Birney published a recent message on slavery by the governor of South Carolina on the front page.[19]

Despite Birney's attempts at moderation, some in the city were not impressed. The *Cincinnati Whig,* which had described the *Philanthropist* as an insult to the city's slaveholding neighbors, called for a meeting to determine what should be done about the newspaper. The meeting was organized by some of the city's most prominent citizens, including the mayor, postmaster, and a former judge of the state supreme court, as well as several lawyers, businessmen, and ministers. Speaker after speaker charged that Birney was a troublemaker who should not be allowed to stir up the city's black population. Some were ready to run the editor out of town, but then he rose to speak. As a native of the South, Birney said he understood the issues that faced the region. The editor maintained that he did not intend to violate any laws in publishing the newspaper and made an eloquent plea for freedom of speech. That apparently was enough for many, and Birney continued to publish the *Philanthropist*.[20]

As a show of support for Birney, the Ohio Anti-Slavery Society agreed to sponsor the journal. Then, during several speaking engagements that spring, protesters sought to silence Birney and others members of the society. At Xenia, Birney was pelted with eggs and rocks. During a speech in Columbus, protesters threw anything they could find at him. Birney said the incidents only fueled his antislavery zeal. "We fight, not with the courage of despair," he wrote, "but with the calmness of certain victory; with the strength of those who feel that their power is from the Almighty; with the weapon of truth prepared by him who is the friend of truth, for the destruction, the final and utter destruction of its adversary, error."[21]

On July 12 a group broke into the office of the *Philanthropist*'s printer and destroyed the next issue of the paper. The handbill soon appeared warning Birney to cease publishing his antislavery views. A few days later, another notice appeared around the city offering a reward of $100 for the "delivery of one *James G. Birney*, a fugitive from justice . . . Said *Birney* in all his associations and feelings is *black*, although his external appearance is white." The action was supported by the *Cincinnati Whig* and the *Cincinnati Republican*. The *Republican* warned the city's antislavery supporters to "eschew the society of James G. Birney" and "avoid him as you would a viper."[22]

When Birney refused to stop publishing, another citywide meeting was held. With the postmaster acting as chairman, a resolution was adopted that recognized "the constitutional right of liberty and speech and of the press," even as it said it was necessary "to utter a warning voice to those concerned in the promulgation of abolition doctrine . . . because we believe their course [is] calculated to inflame the passion of one portion of our yet happy country against the other." Birney and the Ohio Anti-Slavery Society responded that they would not surrender freedom of speech to a group that believed they "possess a power above the law." The editor said the *Philanthropist* had pursued a moderate course in speaking out against slavery and would continue to do so.[23]

But some residents had seen enough. On the evening of July 30 a crowd of residents gathered downtown in front of the Exchange Hotel. In orderly fashion, they elected a chairman and passed resolutions claiming that in the interest of protecting life and property, the *Philanthropist* must be put out of business. The mob then marched down the street to the printing office and carried out their "duty," dragging the press down the street and throwing it into the Ohio River. Afterwards, the mob went to Birney's home planning to tar and feather him. However, the editor was out of town on a lecture trip. Angry at being unable to find Birney, the crowd proceeded to the black section of Cincinnati, where they broke into homes and wrecked a saloon. During the four-hour rampage, no police tried to stop the mob. The mayor stood nearby the entire time and watched silently.[24]

Birney learned about the destruction of the *Philanthropist* on his way home to Cincinnati two days later. Friends convinced him that it was not safe for him to return for several more days. By that time, city officials had the rioters under control. Not surprisingly, the editors of the *Whig* and *Republican* condoned the riot. The *Republican* described it as "the most systematic, orderly, and well behaved mob we have ever witnessed." And the *Whig* remarked that "few seem to be dissatisfied with the result or [have] the slightest sympathy with the sufferers."

But other editors had harsh words for what had taken place in Cincinnati. Birney reprinted editorials from twenty-three newspapers across the country that condemned the mob's action. "We hold that the combination of the few to govern the many by terror of legal violence is as wicked and indefensible as a conspiracy to rob on the highway," said the *New York Evening Post*. The *New York Sun* said the mob established a dangerous precedent, "that a real or pretended opinion of the majority of people should be the governing principle, even though it be in opposition to existing law."[25]

With donations from abolitionist societies and the help of his assistant, Gamaliel Bailey, Birney rebuilt the *Philanthropist,* and the newspaper resumed publishing in the fall. Some of Cincinnati's leading citizens were embarrassed by the violence, and they worked to ease racial tensions in the city. However, Birney had seen enough. The editor soon decided to accept an invitation to move to New York and join the American Anti-Slavery Society as corresponding secretary. Bailey took over as editor of the *Philanthropist* and guided it successfully for seven more years.[26]

Birney and the *Philanthropist* emerged from the ordeal battered but still standing. Tragically, that was not the case for Elijah Lovejoy and his fiery abolitionist journal, the *Observer*. Born in Maine to a Congregationalist preacher and his wife, Lovejoy grew up in a stern Puritanical household where the children were taught to serve God. A serious-minded student, Lovejoy graduated first in his class from Waterville College. As the lands west of the Appalachian Mountains were increasingly being settled, Protestant clergy of the east worried that settlers would not receive a proper religious education there. They encouraged pious church members to move to the new communities of the west to help spread the message of God. The young Lovejoy seemed ideally suited for the task, and after graduation he traveled west, eventually settling in St. Louis. There Lovejoy started his own private high school patterned on classical academies back in the east. The school was successful, but after two years the ambitious Lovejoy wanted to do more.[27]

The publisher of the *St. Louis Times* was looking for a new partner. Lovejoy sold his school and in 1830 joined the newspaper's staff. Missouri was a slaveholding territory. The *Times* regularly printed slave advertisements, and a young black boy owned by a local slaveholder worked in the office. None of this apparently bothered Lovejoy. However, the young man had remained faithful to his religious upbringing, and in 1831 he began attending revival meetings at the First Presbyterian Church. The following year, Lovejoy became a Presbyterian, and soon after that he sold his stake in the paper and left school to attend the Princeton Theological Seminary.

Although Lovejoy preached at a church in New York City for a time, he soon felt pulled back to the west. In 1833 a group of wealthy St. Louis residents wanted to start a reform paper, and they asked Lovejoy to edit it. On November 22, 1833, the first issue of the *St. Louis Observer* appeared. Lovejoy, who continued to be known as "Reverend," announced that he would devote himself to "Christian politics, the diffusion of religious intelligence, and the salvation of souls." Although the newspaper would not seek out controversy, he wrote, it would not run away from it. Whatever the consequences, the *Observer* would "never shrink from the post of duty; nor fear to speak out."[28]

Lovejoy initially was mild in his criticism of slavery. He criticized the tactics of many abolitionists, calling them "the worst enemies the poor slaves have." He also said it was wrong to refer to slave owners as "robbers" and "murderers" and that such talk simply antagonized the South. By 1835, however, Lovejoy had become more outspoken in his criticism of slavery. Other newspapers in the city began to condemn Lovejoy for his views, warning that Southerners would no longer want to settle in the city. They also hinted that abolitionist talk might incite slave insurrections.[29]

When Lovejoy published the statement of principles of the American Anti-Slavery Society and announced his agreement with them, it was too much for some who financially supported the newspaper. Along with other prominent citizens, they sent Lovejoy a letter requesting that he immediately cease his criticism of slavery. However, the increasingly bold Lovejoy refused to back down. He maintained his rights "as a republican citizen, free-born of these United States," to defend fearlessly "the cause of TRUTH AND RIGHTEOUSNESS." He also said he would remain in St. Louis and continue his attacks on slavery. "The path of duty lies plain before me," he wrote, "and I must walk therein, even though it lead . . . to the stake."[30]

In early 1836, Lovejoy published his most zealous editorial against slavery. "Our creed," he declared, "is that slavery is a *sin*—now, heretofore, hereafter, and forever, a sin." Surprisingly, there was little reaction to Lovejoy's criticism, but in April a black man was arrested for allegedly murdering a white. Despite pleas that he should stand trial, a mob broke into the man's jail cell, tied him to a tree, and burned him to death. A horrified Lovejoy condemned the mob in an editorial entitled "Awful Murder and Savage Barbarity." Some members of the group were arrested and brought before a grand jury. The presiding judge, Luke E. Lawless, used the occasion to attack abolitionist literature and pointed to the *Observer* as a clear example. He also instructed the grand jury not to return an indictment if they found the mob was provoked by "electric frenzy." If this was the case, the judge said, then the matter "transcends your jurisdiction—it is beyond the reach of human law." The grand jury did not indict the group's members.[31]

Lovejoy railed against the mob and Judge Lawless. He said that the judge's argument regarding violence meant that "every man must hold his property and his life, at the point of the dagger." The evening that the *Observer*'s editorial appeared, a crowd of about 200 people surrounded the newspaper's office. They broke in and destroyed $700 in printing supplies. Facing such threats, Lovejoy decided he could no longer live safely in St. Louis. He believed that Alton, Illinois, across the Mississippi River, would be more welcoming, so he put his press and printing equipment on a steamboat and sent them across the river. However, word soon spread about what Lovejoy was doing, and before the press could be moved from the wharf in Alton, a group of local men threw it into the river.[32]

With help from the Presbyterian synod of Illinois, Lovejoy purchased a new press. And in the first issue of the new *Alton Observer,* he showed no sign that he was retreating from his pointed criticism of slavery. Lovejoy soon called for a convention to form a state antislavery society. Such talk was too much for many in Alton, who met to see what could be done about the editor. They were joined by the *Missouri Republican,* which had become increasingly critical of Lovejoy. In one editorial, the newspaper said that the editor had "forfeited all claims to the protection of that or any other community." In August 1837, a small group of men gathered outside the *Observer*'s office and began throwing rocks through the windows and shouting insults at the staff. When no police arrived, the staff fled. The group then broke into the office and destroyed the press and other equipment.[33]

Lovejoy was determined not to give in to the violence, and he decided to make a public appeal for financial support to rebuild the paper. With the help of the *Alton Telegraph,* he prepared an extra edition of the *Observer* in the form of a letter addressed to the "Friends and Subscribers of the Alton Observer." It urged all "friends of law and order" to "let the experiment be fairly tried whether the freedom of speech and of the press is to be enjoyed in Illinois or not." Supporters across the country sent Lovejoy contributions, but it was also clear that Alton had become divided over the abolitionist newspaper. The editor was out of town in mid-September when a new press arrived. A group of friends picked up the press and took it to a warehouse for storage until Lovejoy's return. Wary of mob action, the mayor posted a constable outside the warehouse. But the constable left late in the evening, and afterward a group of about twenty men broke in, wrecking the press and throwing it into the river.[34]

Soon after Lovejoy returned, a group of men broke into his home and ordered him to leave the city. At the insistence of his family he fled, but he returned the next day. The editor began sleeping with a loaded rifle. Tensions worsened when an antislavery convention that Lovejoy had helped organize began in Alton. A mob interrupted a speech by abolitionist Edward Beecher, and Lovejoy's house was attacked twice. On one occasion, Lovejoy returned home to find his wife and son in the attic hiding from a group that had tried to break in. Meanwhile, everyone waited for the arrival of another press, which was being shipped from Cincinnati. Lovejoy appealed to the mayor and city council of Alton for protection, but they took no action. Instead, a council member moved that the "Mayor and Common Council address a note to Mr. Lovejoy and his friends, requesting them to relinquish the idea of establishing an abolitionist press at this time." Lovejoy organized his own group to protect the press. On November 5, the *Observer*'s fourth press arrived on a steamship and was stored in a nearby warehouse.

Word quickly spread, and a group of men met at a popular saloon to make plans to destroy the press. When the mob arrived at the warehouse, they began throwing rocks at the windows and doors. Someone fired a gun, and Lovejoy's defenders answered. A young man in the crowd was hit and mortally wounded. The mayor then arrived and appealed for calm. But the mob, incensed that someone had been shot, refused to go away. The mayor then went inside the warehouse and urged Lovejoy and his supporters to leave. In the meantime, the crowd had found a ladder and someone climbed to the roof to set it afire. Several of the defenders rushed out of the building and fired at the mob. With the roof on fire, Lovejoy and another man came out of the building and aimed their pistols at the mob. Both men were hit by gunshots, Lovejoy five times. He fell back into the building, dead. With Lovejoy dead and the building on fire, the defenders fled. The mob entered the warehouse and threw the *Observer*'s press into the Mississippi River one final time.[35]

Lovejoy's death at the hands of a mob shocked the country. The *Colored American*'s headline declared "The Spirit of Slavery Triumphant!!!" and said Lovejoy had been killed "because he dared to lift up his voice against the oppression of the poor slave." The *Emancipator* issued an extra edition; other abolitionist editors framed the announcement in their newspapers with black borders. All proclaimed Lovejoy the first martyr to the abolitionist cause. They also decried how mob violence was threatening cherished American freedoms. "Our country seems fast verging on a revolution," said the *Philanthropist*. "The mob is determined to assert its supremacy; it has a passion for ruling; it has begun a new era—an era marked by the blackest of crimes—the crime of MURDER; and now what shall stay its course or limit its demands!" Some mainstream newspapers, even those with no abolitionist sympathies, also expressed outrage at the killing. "Tis true the course of abolitionists is disgusting to our moral feelings," said the *New Hampshire Statesman,* "but they, like all others, have the right to speak and print what they please." "We trust this horrible affair will have the effect to awaken the people of this country to the danger of mob rule," declared the *Boston Times,* "and to the necessity of maintaining inviolate those laws which are the same to all, and without which no man or woman is safe from personal violence."[36]

Benjamin Lundy and his newspaper did not escape the violence of the decade. The editor, who had published the *Genius of Universal Emancipation* irregularly while traveling to enlist support for colonization, finally closed the newspaper for good in 1836. However, the determined Lundy was not ready to give up antislavery agitation, and that same year he started a new abolitionist weekly in Philadelphia, the *National Enquirer and Constitutional Advocate of Universal Liberty.* The paper's long name was not its only problem. As was the case with the *Genius,* the *National Enquirer* was started with insufficient funds and soon was in financial trouble. The following year, the Pennsylvania Anti-Slavery Society assumed financial responsibility for the publication. The paper later was renamed simply the *Pennsylvania Freeman.*[37]

By this time Lundy was suffering from health problems. In 1838 he announced he was resigning from the paper in order to move closer to his children, now living in Illinois. Seventeen years after starting the *Genius,* Lundy wrote that "I must now look somewhat to the affairs of my own house." Whittier, who had worked on behalf of the abolitionist movement while he continued writing his popular poetry, was named editor of the *Pennsylvania Freeman*. As he prepared to leave Philadelphia, Lundy moved out of his boardinghouse and stored his belongings in the Anti-Slavery Society's offices in Pennsylvania Hall. The impressive new building, dedicated to freedom of speech, had just been built with public donations to provide a meeting place for various reform groups, including the society.[38]

Two days after the dedication of Pennsylvania Hall on May 14, 1838, an antislavery women's convention began meeting in the hall, with both whites and blacks in attendance. Speakers included Garrison, Maria Weston Chapman, Lucretia Mott, and Abby Kelly. An angry crowd gathered to protest the racially mixed meeting, and in the interest of maintaining peace, the mayor ordered the hall closed. However, that evening rioters broke down the doors and set the hall on fire. Whittier managed to save some of his papers by dressing in disguise, mingling with the crowd, and entering the building before it was burned. But all of Lundy's belongings were destroyed by rioters who broke into the Anti-Slavery Society's office. Lundy, who arrived at the hall while the fire was still smoldering, later wrote to his friend John Quincy Adams, "Methought I could read, on this mighty scroll, the woeful destiny of this nation of oppressors."[39]

The pioneering Lundy, who had once written that "neither the powers of earth or hell can move me from my purpose, until the lamp of life shall be extinguished," died a year later in Illinois. Free blacks in Philadelphia, Boston, and other cities held services honoring him. Tributes and memorials praised his tireless work on behalf of the antislavery cause. Garrison published a long, heartfelt obituary in the *Liberator* reviewing

Lundy's career and extolling his mentor. No one in the abolitionist movement, Garrison wrote, "labored more assiduously or surmounted more formidable obstacles, or exhibited more courage . . . or deserves to be held in more grateful and abiding remembrance" than his old friend.[40]

By the time of Lundy's death, the violence that had seemed to envelop the decade was subsiding. Other abolitionist newspapers and their editors would be threatened or attacked, but not to the extent of the hostility seen in the 1830s. The repressive tactics used against abolitionists and their publications had created a sizable coalition of antislavery sympathizers who were concerned with preserving freedom of speech and other civil liberties. Still, the attacks on abolitionists had convinced some antislavery leaders that moral suasion did not work and that new tactics were needed by the movement. With the support of some newspapers, abolitionists began a controversial move into the political arena.

FOUR

WRESTLING WITH QUESTIONS

In the summer of 1837, the *Liberator* published an eloquent series of letters by an abolitionist from South Carolina, Sarah Grimké. Sarah and her sister, Angelina, were rising stars of the abolitionist lecture circuit, where they attracted large audiences with their firsthand knowledge of slavery and their passionate calls to end the institution. However, Sarah's letters published in the *Liberator* dealt not so much with the evils of slavery as with the "equality of the sexes." She declared that God had made no moral distinction between the sexes and that "whatsoever it is morally right for a man to do, it is morally right for a woman to do." Not surprisingly, her views were fully supported by the *Liberator's* editor.[1]

For conservative New England clergy, Grimké's letters in the newspaper were more than they could stand. They drew up a pastoral response criticizing reformers for introducing "agitating subjects" to their congregations and deploring the lack of deference to the pastoral office. They also warned of the dangers which seemed "to threaten the female character" by leading women to transcend "the modesty of [their] sex." A few weeks later, a group of ministers published an attack on the man who had provided the forum for Grimké's letters and who himself had been critical of the clergy. For more than a year, William Lloyd Garrison had condemned church leaders for what he considered their lack of support for the abolitionist cause. A furious Garrison responded to the clerical criticism with a front-page editorial in the *Liberator* declaring that he would bow to no one. He said if it required the downfall of "man-enslaving religion" in order to abolish slavery, that would be perfectly acceptable. A redeemed "spiritual house" would arise from the ruins of the disgraced religious denominations, he predicted.[2]

By 1837 abolitionists were wrestling with ideological questions that were increasingly dividing their ranks. What stance should the movement take toward religious denominations that refused to endorse ending slavery? How should violence be addressed as a response to slavery? What role should women play in the antislavery movement? And the most divisive question of all: what should be the role of party politics in the abolitionist movement? These ideological battles, which overshadowed everything else in the movement until it split in 1840, were played out repeatedly in the pages of the abolitionist press. Garrison used the *Liberator* to continue his war with orthodox New England clergymen, to support pacifism, to call for women to take a more active role in the antislavery movement, and to urge his supporters to avoid politics altogether. Other antislavery papers fought Garrison on many of these issues, arguing that radical ideas were hurting the cause by alienating many supporters.[3]

Elijah Lovejoy's death in defending his newspaper from the Illinois mob put the issue of pacifism front and center. Garrison argued that it was time for abolitionists to declare how far they were willing to go in practicing nonresistance. In the editor's case, it was clear he was willing to go to extraordinary lengths. The first American peace societies were organized early in the nineteenth century, largely in response to the continental wars of the Napoleonic period and their extension to the United States with the War of 1812. The American Peace Society was founded in 1828, absorbing many of the smaller groups, but its approach was too conservative for some in the movement, including Garrison. At the beginning of 1838, Garrison proclaimed in the *Liberator* that "next to the overthrow of slavery, the cause of PEACE will command our attention." He called for the total abrogation of force and argued that any organization or government that depended on the use of violence was illegitimate.[4]

Later that year, Garrison helped establish the New England Non-Resistance Society, a radical group which disavowed all human government. The society's Declaration of Sentiments, penned by Garrison with "all the fanaticism of [his] head and heart," projected a vision of Christian utopia. It proclaimed that neither individuals nor nations had a right to self-defense. Until the day when the government renounced war, its leaders announced, the society would withhold its allegiance from the government. With his usual bravado, Garrison used the *Liberator* to hail the society's declaration. It did not matter that only 26 of the original 160 members of the society signed the declaration. "The progress of Christianity through the world, since the time when only twelve persons were found willing to take up the cross . . . should teach . . . that it is of no consequence how many or how few subscribed to the principles and doctrines of the Declaration," he wrote. The optimism of the society's convention reminded Garrison of the abolitionist movement's early days. He also believed that nonresistance threw "a new light upon the atrocities of slavery and provided a new means of exposing them to the country.[5]

As he always did with controversial subjects, Garrison gave space in the *Liberator* to his critics—and then immediately responded to them. A Methodist minister from Vermont argued that the new organization was not a peace society but a "no-government" group dedicated to civil disobedience. "With your views, I cannot conceive by what authority you appoint officers in your society," the minister wrote. Moreover, how could Garrison recommend the use of petitions if he believed "the very existence of a legislative body to be a sin" while nonetheless "asking of it legislative action"? In his reply, Garrison declared that the end of human government did not mean chaos but the coming of a new order. He also continued to write in the *Liberator* about the need for perfectionism, often basing his arguments on scripture. "The present governments of the world are the consequence of disobedience to the commands of God," he wrote. "We are for subverting the rotten, unequal, anti-Christian government of man, and establishing, as a substitute that which is divine."[6]

Garrison's nonresistance philosophy even went so far as to renounce the act of voting as sinful. Although he stressed that those whose conscience permitted them to cast ballots should continue voting, his fellow abolitionist editors assailed the *Liberator*'s editor. "To talk of being an abolitionist and not in favor of political action against slavery, is a contradiction in terms," wrote William Goodell, editor of the *Friend of Man,* the organ of the New York State Anti-Slavery Society. Joshua Leavitt printed James Birney's "Letter on the Political Obligation of Abolitionists" in the *Emancipator.* Garrison was furious, and he condemned the paper for its "prostitution to party purposes."[7]

But Garrison's running battle with orthodox New England clergymen caused even more controversy. Garrison had become disillusioned with the church, disappointed by men of God whom he believed had turned their backs on many of the important issues of the day, especially slavery. As John L. Thomas has written, Garrison "had grown up with the evangelical belief that churches were God's agents for purifying society . . . As voluntary associations of true Christians the churches ought to lead the way in reforming society." Although some clerics had become abolitionists, many more stayed at arm's length from the movement. Garrison denounced ministers who refused to support antislavery lecturers, some of whom were women, when they tried to speak in their churches. This was just one more indication, he believed, of how the church too often put doctrine ahead of good works. Garrison's criticism of the church went so far as to call into question clerical authority over congregations—and he even repudiated the institution of the Sabbath. Garrison said he found no scriptural authority for the divine origin of the Sabbath, and he questioned the idea of making "the outward observance of one day of the week . . . of paramount importance to every thing else in the moral and spiritual world, instead of being subordinate and cooperative." He went on to write, "Let men consecrate to the service of Jehovah not merely one day in seven, but *all* their time, thought, actions and powers."[8]

The divisions that Garrison often provoked with his views about such issues—and his use of the *Liberator* to spread those opinions—had long concerned some abolitionist leaders. In an open letter to Garrison published in the *Liberator,* John Greenleaf Whittier deplored side issues which he claimed distracted the movement from its main goal. Writing later in the *Pennsylvania*

Freeman, Whittier said, "As abolitionists we have a single object: let us keep eyes single toward it." Before his death, Benjamin Lundy had sharply rebuked his former editorial partner. He criticized Garrison for "arrogance" and for injecting "wild and absurd theories" into the abolitionist movement. Lundy said Garrison's "harsh language, denunciatory style and . . . spirit of dogmatism" hurt the cause. The *Philanthropist's* Gamaliel Bailey said the antislavery cause had brought together men of various religious and political views. When Garrison raised controversial issues, it could only lead to discord among abolitionists, which could "contravene the sole object of their union." For the sake of unity, Bailey said antislavery editors should exclude all extraneous subjects from their publications.[9]

By 1839 conservative leaders had seen enough and were making plans to dislodge the Garrisonians from the Massachusetts Anti-Slavery Society. They planned to dispose of the "women question" by refusing to seat female delegates at the Massachusetts society's upcoming convention and then gain control of the *Liberator.* Garrison learned of the plan and used the newspaper to respond. "Strong foes are without, insidious plotters are within the camp," he warned. "A conflict is at hand . . . which is to be more hotly contested, and which will require more firmness of nerve and greater singleness of purpose . . . than any through which we have passed to victory."[10]

At the society's annual meeting, Garrison's critics presented two resolutions: one calling for the establishment of an independent weekly publication for the state society, and the second making the *Liberator* that organ. Supporters of the moves criticized Garrison for his nonresistance principles and said the newspaper was ignoring political matters important to abolitionism. In arguing for the resolutions, Henry B. Stanton attacked the "nullifying effects" of perfectionism on the abolitionist cause and the fact that the *Liberator* was used to spread the heresy. "It is not that other subjects are introduced into the *Liberator*," the New Yorker declared, "it is that *such* other subjects are introduced, subjects so injurious to the cause." The society must have a publication that could be counted on to support the abolitionist agenda and that agenda alone, Stanton argued. Garrison defended his controversial views and claimed he never insisted that everybody agree with them. In the end, his supporters marshaled enough support to vote down the resolutions.

In an editorial published after the meeting, Garrison wrote that the "good ship *Abolition*" had survived "the most violent gale recorded in her log-book, to the imminent peril of her existence, and not without injury to her spars and rigging, and the loss of some of her crew." He concluded bitterly, "The antislavery house in this Commonwealth is now divided against itself—and how can it stand?—What its most powerful enemies could not do, is now to be effected by the treachery of its former friends." Unable to gain control of the *Liberator*, Garrison's opponents started a new publication, the *Massachusetts Abolitionist*. It derided Garrison as "the reformer-general of humanity" and rebuked the Massachusetts society for becoming "a woman's rights, no-government organization."[11]

The antagonism between abolitionist leaders continued and, as usual with the movement, it was played out in the press. Years earlier, the American Anti-Slavery Society had agreed not to solicit funds in areas organized by state societies. However, as the state societies grew, the area where the national society had jurisdiction became smaller and smaller. As a result, the American Anti-Slavery Society became increasingly dependent on the state societies for financial support. In 1840 Garrison announced that the Massachusetts society would no longer provide financial support for the national society, even though it was in financial trouble. Writing in the *Liberator,* he blamed the American Anti-Slavery Society's executive committee, claiming there was "a growing distrust in their clear-sightedness, sound judgment, rigid impartiality, and anti-sectarian spirit."[12]

At the same time, Garrison was increasingly critical of Leavitt's leadership of the *Emancipator,* the society's newspaper. In an April editorial in the *Liberator,* he called for Leavitt's resignation. Garrison said he appreciated Leavitt's "editorial tact and ability," but he no longer had "that clearness of vision and freedom of soul" needed to be editor. Leavitt responded angrily in the *Emancipator* that he was guided by his own conscience on antislavery issues and that he would not be anyone's mouthpiece. He called Garrison's *Liberator* "a self-constituted 'organ,' irresponsible, arbitrary, and allowing no appeal from its decrees."[13]

In private correspondence with one another, some leaders of the society decried what Garrison was doing. Gerrit Smith, a wealthy philanthropist and abolitionist supporter, complained of the editor's "coarse, unprovoked [and] wanton attack . . . on the motives of his brethren." Arthur Tappan's brother, Lewis, called Garrison "the Massachusetts madman" and said he was leading the American Anti-Slavery Society to ruin. "We are now a sad spectacle to the nation," Tappan wrote. "The predictions of opponents seems to be about to be verified. They said we were a fanatical set of men, that we could not stick together, that the concern would soon be blown up."[14]

The New York leaders of the American Anti-Slavery Society finally resolved to purge the organization of its radical elements and renounce their doctrines. When Garrison learned what they were planning, he used the *Liberator* to issue a counter-manifesto. He claimed the society was threatened by a select group that would take it down the wrong path in its fight against slavery. The group, he wrote, "has thrown its mask aside, and unblushingly declares that our sacred cause cannot be safely trusted in the hands of 'the common people'—the farmers, mechanics, and workingmen—but must be placed under the control of a select body of men in order to give it respectability and success!" Garrison urged his supporters to pack the society's annual meeting, and he even went so far as to make special arrangements with railroad and steamship companies for New Englanders to travel at lower rates. "In whatever part of the country you reside, we call you to rally the meeting as one man," he declared. Garrison's supporters responded to the call. More than 400 packed a steamship, taking every available berth, and when those were filled, spreading blankets on the floor. During the voyage they held a deckside rally that included speeches and songs.[15]

Garrison's rivals had rallied their own supporters. In all, more than 1,000 delegates attended the opening of the American Anti-Slavery Society's convention on May 12, 1840, at the Fourth Free Church in New York City. The first task was the nomination of a business committee that would fix the meeting's agenda. To no one's surprise, the Garrisonians nominated Abby Kelley, an outspoken feminist and close associate of the editor. When she was elected by a vote of 571 to 451, angry opponents led by Lewis Tappan refused to stand for it. They claimed it would be "promiscuous" to conduct the society's business affairs with a woman on the business committee. Moreover, it would defy scripture and fly in the face of societal customs.

The following day, opponents of Garrison set up a rival organization, the American and Foreign Anti-Slavery Society. The 300 members of the new society adopted a constitution that urged, among other projects, the organization of women's auxiliary antislavery societies. Arthur Tappan was elected president, James Birney and Stanton secretaries, and Lewis Tappan treasurer.[16]

The Garrisonians, or the "old organization," as they now called themselves, passed resolutions censuring the secessionists and denouncing the church as "the foe of freedom, humanity and pure religion, so long as it occupies its present position." They elected Lucretia Mott, Maria Weston Chapman, and Lydia Maria Child, as well as a black leader, Thomas Van Rensselaer, to the new executive committee. "We have made clean work of everything," Garrison bragged in a letter to his wife after the meeting concluded.[17]

The founders of the new society took the *Emancipator* with them, so the Garrisonians founded a new weekly abolitionist publication, the *National Anti-Slavery Standard*. Nathaniel Rogers agreed to serve as editor. The *Standard* carried the front-page motto "Without Concealment—Without Compromise." The new publication denounced Tappan as a narrow-minded sectarian who had tried to force religious conservatism and partisan politics on the society. The *Standard,* it claimed, was proof that the "old organization" remained active and had not surrendered to the "new organization." Rogers declared the new society to be a greater enemy of the antislavery cause than slave owners. Responding to critics of the old organization's radical views, the *Standard* said members had "no *right* to compromise the laws of eternal Justice. We cannot forsake the counsels of Omniscient Wisdom to follow after those of mercenary demagogues in church or state."[18]

As the American Anti-Slavery Society was splitting apart, moderate abolitionist leaders turned their attention to creating a third political party. In 1839 a group of abolitionists under the leadership of Myron Holley, the antislavery editor of the *Rochester Freeman,* organized a series of small gatherings to persuade supporters to nominate independent candidates for the upcoming presidential election. Holley and others did not get far. However, when it became apparent by the spring of 1840 that Martin Van Buren and William Henry Harrison were going to be the nominees of the Democratic and Whig parties respectively, efforts intensified to nominate a third-party ticket.[19]

Abolitionist editors wrestled with what a third party, dedicated to overthrowing slavery, would mean to the antislavery movement. Some feared that the drive for political office would destroy the moral foundations of the cause. "No reformer can make use of political machinery, as a means to effect his ends, without moral injury to himself, and serious detriment to the cause he advocates," the *Anti-Slavery Standard* editorialized. Editors also claimed that an antislavery party would not stand a chance against the major parties. The *Emancipator*'s Leavitt initially supported these arguments, but after a "long and earnest mental struggle" he endorsed the idea of an independent ticket. The major parties opposed abolition and so abolitionists were effectively disenfranchised, he argued. Since moral suasion had failed, the only option was to elect candidates who would support the goals of the antislavery movement.[20]

Not surprisingly, Garrison opposed the formation of a third party to fight slavery. He argued that societal changes were accomplished by God's truth, not by corrupt political parties. The editor said that moral suasion was working and there was no need for abolitionists to abandon it for the political arena. "Why should we alter our course? If God be with us, who can be against us?" he wrote in the *Liberator*. "Who will be so impious as to contend that he will forsake us, frown upon us . . . if we refuse to organize ourselves into a political party? Let us not countenance any such movement—it is pregnant with corruption and defeat."[21]

However, third-party supporters persisted and announced plans for a convention in Albany, New York, on April 1, 1840. The 120 delegates nominated a presidential ticket headed by former *Philanthropist* editor Birney to run under the banner of the new Liberty Party. Garrison called the Albany meeting the "April Fool's Convention" and dismissed the small number of delegates attending as a joke. "A National Convention, forsooth!" he wrote. "Why, it was not as large as a common village meeting!" Garrison claimed that Birney and Stanton were building an independent party for their own selfish purposes. After being defeated for control of the American Anti-Slavery Society, they had turned to political means to achieve their goals, he argued. Other abolitionist editors fired back, saying that Garrison secretly favored Harrison in the race. Goodell, editor of the *Friend of Man,* published a biting satire about Garrison, entitled "How to Make a Pope." Take a strong-minded leader, surround him with unquestioning friends, and soon he will believe that he is infallible. That is how it had been with the bishops of Rome and that is how it was now with Garrison, Goodell wrote.[22]

During the 1840 campaign, the *Emancipator* devoted considerable space to Liberty Party news. Leavitt wrote repeated editorials on why abolitionists should abandon the major parties and support a third-party ticket. Leavitt, in fact, became one of the party's organizational leaders. He helped set up rallies, parades, and picnics. He served on the party's national committee and arranged conventions, hired speakers, and raised funds for the party. He also started a separate Liberty Party campaign news paper. By this point, the animosity between Garrison and Leavitt had become so great that Garrison was regularly putting *Emancipator* editorials in the "Refuge of Oppression" column of the *Liberator,* a place usually reserved for material from proslavery newspapers.[23]

For his part, Gamaliel Bailey had been touting the need for political action for years in the *Philanthropist,* which he edited. Beginning in 1839, he argued for a broad-based liberal party as the political arm of the antislavery movement. But he initially objected to the idea of a strictly abolitionist party. Whittier, Leavitt, and others criticized this view, and finally Bailey came around to their way of thinking. Now the *Philanthropist* issued a call to "unite patriots, philanthropists and Christians, to put down the slavery of all parties, and put up the principles of the Declaration of Independence, at the ballot box." Bailey used a biblical analogy in responding to those who said an independent ticket was not yet needed: "How long would it have taken the Apostles to 'Christianize the public mind,' had they continued to practice idolatry while preaching against it?" The editor accused Garrisonians of doing the "dirty work" of the parties by "circulating groundless slanders and malignant personal abuse" against Liberty Party candidates.[24]

As the 1840 campaign came to an end, the Liberty Party's supporters in the abolitionist press recognized that they had been unable to convince most antislavery voters to abandon the major parties. Party attachments were so strong, Leavitt complained, that "it is almost like plucking out a right eye, or off a right arm, for one who has mingled much in party strife, and enjoyed the confidence of political associates, to cut loose and pronounce his party corrupt." Harrison narrowly defeated Van Buren, while Birney received a tiny 7,000 votes.

Abolitionist editors who supported the new party tried to put the best face on the defeat and emphasized the long-term effects of the independent ticket. Leavitt argued in the *Emancipator* that Liberty candidates "had more effect in preparing the way for the abolition of slavery, yes, tenfold more than all the rest [of the abolitionists] put together." Bailey claimed that the immediate purpose of an independent ticket was to influence the Democrats and Whigs to accept antislavery principles. But he also hoped that the result would be the formation of a party "based on the grand doctrine of human rights proclaimed in the Declaration of Independence."[25]

For his part, Garrison was relieved when the election was over. To him the results of the election were clear evidence that a third party could not be effective. If the Whigs and Democrats "cannot be converted by moral-suasion, it is perfectly plain that the third party will forever constitute a most insignificant minority and thus fail to accomplish its object. If they can be, then this new party is as needless as a fifth wheel to a coach."[26]

Garrison continued attacking the Liberty Party as it tried to rebound after the disappointing showing in 1840. When Birney agreed to lead the party, Garrison accused him of being Leavitt's "dupe" and a man "not to be relied on in cases of strong temptation." He called Birney's followers "vandal enemies" who had abandoned the right course of abolitionism because of the "miserable jealousy" of its leaders. Garrison implied that the goal of the Liberty Party was not to end slavery but to oust him from the movement. The party was an organization "conceived in sin," Garrison wrote, and as such "the most dangerous foes with which genuine anti-slavery has to contend."[27]

But as the Liberty Party steadily grew, Garrison changed his tone and admitted some success for the party. "We have never opposed the formation of a third party as a measure inherently wrong," he wrote in 1841, "but we have always contended that the abolitionists have as clear and indisputable right to band themselves together as those who call themselves whigs or democrats." He argued that an antislavery party was not needed at a time when so much "preliminary toil" needed to be done by the movement's members. "When a nation is to be reformed, the first thing *in order,* is to arouse it from its slumber of mortal death; and when this is accomplished . . . the reformation may be said to have made a mighty stride forward," he wrote. He continued to argue that abolitionists could not improve on the "apostolic mode" of changing corrupt institutions. In answering the question, *"How shall the people be brought to repentance?"* Garrison argued as he had always done: "Moral suasion . . . is the mode appointed by God to conquer error, and destroy the works of darkness."

During the next several years, the abolitionist press continued to debate the usefulness of political parties to the antislavery cause. For his part, Garrison considered both Whigs and Democrats "a terrible curse to the land." He argued that the only reason why the two parties did not support the abolitionist cause was because "the people of the land are pro-slavery." The way to end slavery, he maintained as he always did, was "a moral change in the people . . . Truth no more relies for success on ballot boxes than it does on cartridge boxes . . . Political action is not moral action, any more than a box on the ear is an argument."[28]

Although widespread violence had subsided, abolitionist newspapers continued to suffer from occasional violence at the hands of groups who did not like what they were fomenting. In 1841 the *Philanthropist* was targeted again. Bailey, the *Philanthropist* editor who succeeded Birney, had kept the paper on a moderate course ever since the paper had been greeted so violently upon its founding in Cincinnati. The son of a Methodist Episcopal minister, Bailey had grown up near Philadelphia and took medical courses with the plan of becoming a doctor. But before starting a medical practice he became editor of the *Methodist Protestant*. The church newspaper was published in Baltimore, and while in the city Bailey witnessed slavery for the first time. He soon became a major supporter of the American Colonization Society. Bailey developed a candid, persuasive prose style as editor of the *Methodist Protestant*. He did not write about slavery often and when he did, he described it as "an evil not of *choice* but of necessity." The conservative Bailey refused to condemn slaveholders, but he urged them to see the error of their ways. Although he believed blacks were entitled to their freedom, he did not believe they deserved the same rights as whites.[29]

Bailey decided to go to Cincinnati, where his parents had moved a year earlier. There his interest in the antislavery movement grew. The conservative views he espoused in Baltimore evolved and he became a convert to the immediatism preached by Garrison. He also got to know Theodore Weld, a young abolitionist and one of the leaders of the Lane Theological Seminary, which became a hotbed of antislavery sentiment. Weld believed that the only effective way to end slavery was to convince owners to free their slaves, a viewpoint that Bailey shared. Bailey became active in the Cincinnati Anti-Slavery Society and was named its secretary. With his background in journalism, he took a great interest when James Birney moved to the city to start the *Philanthropist.* As secretary of the local antislavery society, he was an obvious choice to become Birney's assistant when the state society agreed to sponsor the newspaper. When Birney left Cincinnati after the paper was attacked in 1836, Bailey became editor.

Racial tensions had been simmering in Cincinnati after the Ohio Supreme Court ruled that slaves brought into the state voluntarily by their masters were free under state law. Southerners who did business in the city traditionally brought their servants with them, and after the ruling some slaves fled, taking refuge in the city's black neighborhood. City leaders worried that Cincinnati might lose its lucrative economic ties with the South. On September 3, 1841, a group of whites planned to assault homes and businesses in the black neighborhood, but residents armed to defend themselves. Some community leaders, including the *Cincinnati Enquirer,* blamed abolitionists for the blacks' militancy. The following night, a mob attacked the *Philanthropist* office and threw the press into the river. Bailey managed to escape any harm.[30]

Individuals and abolitionist groups from across the country sent donations to rebuild the *Philanthropist.* Money even came from the Massachusetts Anti-Slavery Society, which had disagreed with Bailey on many subjects. Garrison and Wendell Phillips wrote Bailey that although they often differed over tactics, they "never doubted the purity of your motives" and "highly appreciated your editorial candor and ability." Bailey had the press replaced, and the *Philanthropist* was soon publishing again.[31]

The *Philanthropist* had always struggled financially. Although the mob action garnered the newspaper national attention, it did not attract many new subscribers. While the *Philanthropist* had remained the official publication of the Ohio Anti-Slavery Society, Bailey often angered influential society members with his criticism of Garrison's views on nonresistance, women's rights, and political action. At the state society's annual meeting in 1842, the Garrisonians resigned to form a separate antislavery society, the Western Anti-Slavery Society. Bailey used the opportunity to assume ownership of the *Philanthropist,* with the Ohio Liberty Party and the Ohio Ladies Educational Society agreeing to sponsor the paper. Bailey then took steps to turn around the *Philanthropist*'s financial problems by reaching out to a larger audience. He increased coverage of other reform movements, added business news, and published more fiction. He also cut the annual subscription rate to one dollar. The moves worked. The *Philanthropist*'s circulation, which had never been more than 3,000 in any previous year, jumped to 6,000 by 1845.[32]

However, Garrisonians in the state decided they needed their own publication, and in 1848 they started a new abolitionist publication, the *Anti-Slavery Bugle.* Marius R. Robinson, a longtime abolitionist lecturer and a friend of Bailey, was named editor. The newspaper adopted the *Liberator*'s motto, "No Union with Slaveholders," and promised it would "blow a blast that shall be clear and startling as a hunting horn or a battle charge." The *Anti-Slavery Bugle* followed Garrison's views on most issues. It regularly condemned churches for not supporting abolitionist activities. It claimed that American citizens had every right to renounce their allegiance to a government that supported slavery. The paper also repeatedly criticized Bailey for what it considered his compromises on many moral issues.[33]

Meanwhile, the *Emancipator* also was undergoing changes. By 1841 the newspaper was in serious financial trouble, and the struggling American and Foreign Anti-Slavery Society could not be of much help. Late in the year, Leavitt resigned his position with the society and moved the *Emancipator* to Boston, where he merged it with another newspaper under the auspices of the Massachusetts Abolition Society. In Boston, the *Emancipator* became the Massachusetts organ of the Liberty Party for the next seven years. Until the founding of the *National Era* in 1847, it was the country's leading Liberty paper.[34]

The *Anti-Slavery Standard* was having problems of its own. The American Anti-Slavery Society had been facing a financial crisis before the split, and with many of its major benefactors gone, the organization was constantly on the verge of collapsing. As a result, there was little money to support a newspaper. The *Standard* also suffered from inconsistent leadership. Between 1840 and 1844 the newspaper had three editors—all of whom resigned, at least in part, because of Garrison's dictatorial manner. He demanded editorial control over the paper and did not tolerate anyone who wanted to do anything differently. Child once joked that Garrison's idea of a proper editorial was a preamble with a dozen resolutions and that when the editor went to heaven he would present Saint Peter with resolutions that protested being admitted by a traitor who had betrayed his master.[35]

Nathaniel Rogers lasted just one year as editor of the *Anti-Slavery Standard*. He was succeeded by Child. An accomplished writer of both nonfiction and fiction, Child certainly had the writing credentials for the job. She had also started a children's magazine and helped her husband, David, edit the *Massachusetts*

Journal. She also published a two-hundred-page book, *An Appeal in Favor of that Class of Americans Called Africans,* which described the evil effects of slavery and racial prejudice. During her two years as editor, Child tried to heal the wounds from the society's split. She argued that the abolitionist movement had room for what she called both the "stop there" and "go ahead" factions. In calling for unity, she used a biblical illustration, citing the examples of Peter and Paul. Although the two disciples had different approaches, Child wrote, both were "true to the voice of God" in their souls. She also reminded abolitionists that their duty was the same despite their differences. "The slave still stands in chains, counting the time of his redemption by minutes, while we count it by years," she wrote.[36]

Besides trying to bring the warring factions together, Child sought to attract a broader audience for the newspaper by adding literary and intellectual essays and commentary. She published works by Frances Trollope, Charles Dickens, Alexis de Tocqueville, Nathaniel Hawthorne, and other popular writers. She also started her own column, "Letters from New-York," in which she explored various social problems in the city that crossed racial boundaries, among them poverty, alcoholism, and prejudice. Child believed that by luring readers to the paper "with the garland of imagination and taste," she would induce them to "look candidly" at the issue of slavery.[37]

Child's improvements attracted more readers to the *Anti-Slavery Standard.* By the end of her second year, the paper had about 5,000 readers, twice the number it had when she took over. However, the changes did not sit well with the society's more radical members, including Kelly, Chapman, Rogers, and, of course, Garrison, all of whom wanted her to take a tougher stance on antislavery issues. Child, who adamantly refused to engage in sectarian feuding, could not go along. In her farewell to the *Standard*'s readers, she did not mention her disagreement with the Garrisonian radicals. She just reiterated the editorial approach she had taken with the publication and hinted that she probably was temperamentally unsuited to the job she had undertaken.[38]

Child's husband took over as editor, but he lasted less than a year in the job. The society then turned to a three-pronged arrangement for editing the *Anti-Slavery Standard:* Chapman and Edmund Quincy assumed responsibility for writing the paper's editorials, while Sydney Gay assumed daily management of the paper's office. However, Gay, an abolitionist lecturer from New England, soon took over most of the editorial duties. A talented writer and devoted follower of Garrison, Gay was faithful to many of his views. Most importantly, the mild-mannered and hard-working Gay provided the *Anti-Slavery Standard* with badly needed stability and guided it successfully for the next fourteen years.[39]

The split in the American Anti-Slavery Society did not discourage Garrison from taking controversial positions. Increasingly, he came to believe that disunion was the best way of ending slavery. He argued that people of the free states had to demand a repeal of the Union "not as a threat but as a moral obligation" to purge their souls of guilt. During the gag rule debate in Congress, he addressed an open letter in the *Liberator* to the "desperadoes" of the South, saying that they should simply leave the Union if they would not end slavery. "So far as we are concerned, we 'dissolved the Union' with them, as slaveholders, the first blow we aimed at their nefarious slave system," he wrote. "We do not acknowledge them to be within the pale of Christianity, of republicanism, of humanity." In late 1841, he wrote an editorial about a haunting childhood nightmare of a shipwreck. "It is now settled beyond all controversy, that this nation is out on a storm-tossed sea, without compass, or chart, or rudder, and with the breakers of destruction all around her," he wrote. "They who would be saved must gird themselves with life-preservers, and be prepared to fill the life-boat without delay." Soon Garrison put a new motto on the *Liberator*'s masthead, declaring in capital letters: "A REPEAL OF THE UNION BETWEEN NORTHERN LIBERTY AND SOUTHERN SLAVERY IS ESSENTIAL TO THE ABOLITION OF THE ONE AND THE PRESERVATION OF THE OTHER."[40]

Subsequently, at the annual meeting of the Massachusetts Anti-Slavery Society in 1843, Garrison introduced a remarkable resolution declaring "that the compact which exists between the North and the South is 'a covenant with death, and agreement with hell'—involving both parties in atrocious criminality; and should immediately be annulled." The resolution was adopted, and Garrison began running it at the top of the *Liberator*'s editorial column. By 1844, when the American Anti-Slavery Society met to celebrate its tenth anniversary, Garrison had rewritten the organization's Declaration of Sentiments. Henceforth, the society's rallying cry would be "NO UNION WITH SLAVEHOLDERS!" The declaration committed the society to "cease sustaining the existing compact by withdrawing from the polls, and calmly waiting for a time when a righteous government shall supersede the institutions of tyranny." However, not even the usually persuasive Garrison could convince a majority of the society's members to support such a radical declaration. Nearly half of those in attendance voted against the statements. They also read protests into the meeting's minutes calling Garrison's declaration "impracticable" and "intolerant."[41]

As Henry Mayer has pointed out, the shock value of disunion most appealed to Garrison. Disunion not only put the issue in as stark terms as possible, but it was a unmistakable statement of Garrison's moral priorities. But the idea of breaking up the Union went too far in the view of some antislavery editors. Writing in the *Philanthropist,* Bailey said disunionism was impractical and against the national interest. He argued that it was far better to use "political instrumentalities" to defeat slavery than "simple denunciation . . . unaccompanied by any action." Even the *Anti-Slavery Standard,* now under the editorship of David Child, complained that Garrison was foisting his own dangerous views on the society. Child wrote in the *Standard* before the meeting: "I am in favor of dissolution, if we cannot have abolition; but I could wish to see all reasonable means used of reforming, before we destroy the Constitution."[42]

Garrison refused to back down. He argued that some of the critics were the same people who had objected to the motto of "immediate emancipation." Moreover, he said that all society members did not have to accept the creed. Although members must be in unanimity about the evil of slavery, that could not be expected in the application of their conviction "to existing political institutions." As he often did, Garrison opened the pages of the *Liberator* to attacks on his views. Smith argued that the North was responsible for slavery because it refused to elect an antislavery administration or abolish slavery under federal jurisdiction. The calls for disunion simply relieved Northern consciences by blaming the Constitution for the sins of the North, he wrote. To that Garrison replied that to tell the North to end its alliance with the South was not intended to soothe the region's conscience, but to charge the North with being an accessory to the crime of slavery. "Who advocates a geographical secession, unless it be preceded by a geographical reformation—and how is that secession possible, so long as both parts of the country remain pro-slavery in spirit?" Garrison wrote. "This revolution is to be commenced by *freemen,* carried on by FREEMEN, consummated by FREEMEN."[43]

In the summer of 1842, Garrison published an editorial roll call of his former associates in the abolitionist movement. He asked what had become of men such as Birney, Whittier, Stanton, Theodore Weld, and Elizur Wright, among others—and then proceeded to disparage what each had been doing for the anti-slavery cause lately. It was a typical Garrison editorial and was unfair in many ways. Most of the men he criticized were still working on behalf of the movement, although not in ways that suited the *Liberator*'s cantankerous editor. Yet as Garrison pointed out, the abolitionist cause had indeed splintered into a group of factions. Supporters no longer marched united under the banner of the American Anti-Slavery Society. Instead, abolitionists were divided among Garrisonians, the American and Foreign Anti-Slavery Society, the Liberty Party, and various local and religious groups. Certainly, this state of affairs was reflected in the growing number of abolitionist publications, which some-times seemed to spend as much time battling against one another as they did against slavery. The press feuding would continue throughout the decade. However, these differences took a back seat as the annexation of Texas and a war with Mexico forced the nation to confront the question of slavery's future in the new territories of the west. An increasing number of abolitionist newspapers, including more published by free blacks, weighed in on the debate.[44]

◇

FIVE

NEW PUBLICATIONS

As he sat down to write an editorial for the *Philanthropist* in the spring of 1844, Gamaliel Bailey had read all he could stand about criticism of the abolitionist forces operating in the nation's capital. The Cincinnati editor was convinced that the national press was biased against the antislavery movement and deliberately ignored or misrepresented abolitionist activities. "Shall Slavery be permitted to strike dumb the press, which should glory in being the Press of the Union?" Bailey asked in an editorial. "If so, the sooner we have a free paper in Washington the better."[1]

Bailey was not the only abolitionist leader who believed the cause required a strong presence in the District of Columbia. Three years earlier, Joshua Leavitt and Theodore Weld had established an antislavery lobby in the capital. While ostensibly employed as the *Emancipator*'s congressional reporter, Leavitt spent every session working with members of the House and Senate in fighting against the annexation of Texas, the gag rule, and other issues important to the movement. However, the tireless Leavitt could only do so much. John Greenleaf Whittier and Amos A. Phelps also recognized the problem after a visit to Washington in 1845. They convinced Lewis Tappan that a new national publication could help the cause by transcending sectionalism and reaching into the South. Tappan agreed to support the project, and he tapped Bailey to edit the new publication.[2]

That same year other newspapers joined the growing roster of abolitionist publications, including the first black-owned newspaper to attract a sizable readership, Frederick Douglass's *North Star,* and the first founded by a woman, Jane Grey Swisshelm's *Pittsburgh Saturday Visiter.* The new publications appeared at the same time the antislavery struggle was becoming increasingly political and as the United States went to war with its neighbor, Mexico. The newspapers joined the growing debate over what role the abolitionist movement should play in political parties, including two upstart parties. The newspapers also joined antislavery leaders in decrying the Mexican War as a means of extending slavery into the west and the Compromise of 1850 as a means of avoiding the slavery question.

In choosing Bailey to edit the new national abolitionist publication, Tappan believed he had the man with the temperament to publish a newspaper in Washington. Bailey's forthright editorials against slavery and his courage in facing down mob threats in Cincinnati had earned him praise from many abolitionist leaders. Tappan, who had supported the *Philanthropist* financially for years, also liked Bailey's judicious and moderate approach to many issues. For his part, Bailey was ready for a new editorial challenge. By 1846 the *Philanthropist* was losing subscribers to Ohio's other main abolitionist publication, the *Anti-Slavery Bugle.* Bailey's criticism of disunionism and his support for the Liberty Party had made him unpopular with many Garrisonians in Ohio for what they considered his compromises on moral issues.[3]

The inaugural issue of the *National Era* appeared on January 7, 1847. To some, the name implied that the new publication was to be the national organ of the Liberty Party. Although the paper would support the fledgling party, its founders said, the title was chosen to reflect what they hoped would be a new period in the antislavery struggle, a period in which the movement would expand into the South and become national in scope. Bailey announced in the first issue that a goal of the *National Era* was to present Southerners with "such facts and arguments as may serve to throw further light upon the questions of slavery, and its disposition." The editor argued that many people in the South "feel in their hearts that the haughty claim that slavery shall be exempt from investigation, discussion, opposition, is a gross absurdity." These people, he said, "are willing to listen to discussion, so that they be treated as men whose peculiar circumstances should not be lost sight of and who have minds to be reasoned with, sensibilities to be respected."[4]

Bailey, who had come to know many Southerners from his years in Cincinnati, had long believed that the region's leaders could be convinced to abolish slavery themselves. He emphasized that Southerners should be treated as reasonable people who, if not offended by hostile abolitionist rhetoric and tactics, could be persuaded to act against slavery. To this end, Bailey did everything possible not to offend the region's moderates. Unlike other abolitionist editors, he refused to engage in moral invective. He even stopped using the term *abolitionist* in the *National Era* because he thought it frightened too many people.

Bailey directed the *National Era* at the large non-slaveholding majority in the South. In editorial after editorial Bailey lashed out at the "slave power," arguing that just as there could be no compromise with slavery, there could be no compromise with the slave power. Slaveholders wanted a "complete monopoly of power" in the South, he declared. This monopoly gave the slave owners extraordinary influence in national affairs because the South was united under one class, while the North was divided among various economic groups. Moreover, he argued, the slave power wanted to use its influence to extend slavery not only throughout the western territories but also into Mexico, Central America, and the Caribbean. Bailey warned that unless steps were taken, proslavery forces would eventually gain "perpetual and universal ascendancy." He also argued that ending slavery would free Southerners from domination by slaveholders, raise the price of labor, and provide economic benefits to the region. Bailey bluntly said that Southerners risked a "war of extermination" as long as slavery existed. The answer for the South was peaceful emancipation.[5]

For Bailey, no argument for the economic necessity of slavery could justify the institution. "Well-being can never depend upon wrong-doing," he wrote. "The rights of one class are not to be secured by depriving another class of all rights. Equal justice to all men, of whatever race or color, grade or state, is the only foundation of solid prosperity." Bailey said abolitionists could never compromise or be neutral in the struggle over slavery. "Neutrality is unmanly—nay, worse—it is treason to great interests," he wrote. "If the South is right, we are fearfully wrong—if we are right, the South is fearfully wrong."[6]

Bailey also used the *National Era* to repeatedly call for the better treatment of Washington's free blacks and free blacks in general. He opposed taxes, curfews, and bans on travel that singled out blacks for discriminatory treatment. He protested the legal system that often punished blacks harshly for minor offenses, while not providing them with proper protection from lawbreaking whites. And he regularly criticized racist arguments that blacks were innately inferior to whites.

Bailey became involved in the revival of black emigration schemes in the 1850s. In the past he had been a staunch opponent of the American Colonization Society, writing that supporters of colonization opposed the advancement of blacks in the United States. However, in 1851 Bailey began to advocate voluntary black emigration to Mexico and the West Indies. He argued that migration was a way for blacks to better themselves as white pioneers had done. Bailey condemned the white-only homestead bill meant to encourage settlement in the West as "utterly vulgar" because it denied blacks the same opportunity. He said that blacks needed land in the new territories because they were "excluded by a wicked prejudice from political and professional pursuits." As Bailey's biographer, Stanley Harrold, has pointed out, many complex considerations led him to this view. Bailey came to conclude that the insistence of Southern whites that blacks and whites could not live together peacefully was the main obstacle to the spread of the antislavery movement. He also believed that white prejudice would prevent blacks from achieving equal rights.[7]

The nation's capital at midcentury was a conservative Southern city in many respects. The district was surrounded by slave states, and the slave trade thrived within sight of the Capitol. Many residents were committed to slavery and suspicious of abolitionists. Bailey's wife was snubbed by women in the city, and his children were called "damned abolitionists." Bailey told a fellow editor that he "fully expected to be mobbed," but he was determined to do what he could "by honest management to prevent it." The district's newspapers included the conservative *National Intelligencer,* edited by Joseph Gales and William Seaton, and the staunchly proslavery *Union,* edited by Thomas Ritchie. After moving to Washington, Bailey called on the editors and impressed them with his goodwill. When Ritchie denounced senators who criticized President James K. Polk's conduct of the Mexican War as traitors, and the Senate responded by barring the editor from attending its sessions, Bailey used the *National Era* to defend Ritchie. "What is the liberty press good for if every expression . . . is to be nicely criticized?" Bailey asked.[8]

Tappan envisioned the *National Era* as part of a national organization centered in Washington that would also publish a series of antislavery tracts and books for general circulation. A skilled fund-raiser, he had secured pledges of $63,000 by the time the newspaper began publishing. The funds provided the *National Era* with a comfortable home, something no antislavery newspaper, even the *Liberator,* had enjoyed before. The *National Era* was published from a two-story brick building opposite the patent office and near the center of the capital. The business and publishing departments occupied the first floor, while the editorial and printing departments took up the second. The press was housed in a small building in the rear.

To help pay for its impressive home, Bailey sought to broaden the *National Era*'s appeal by publishing fiction, poetry, and other material of general interest to readers. Whittier, the popular poet who had resigned as editor of the *Pennsylvania Freeman* in 1840, was named literary editor. He secured poetry and prose by William Gallagher, Lydia Maria Child, Oliver Wendell Holmes, Grace Greeenwood, and other popular writers. Whittier himself contributed more than 300 pieces of poetry and prose during his ten years with the newspaper. The *National Era* also carried editorials on antislavery and other reform movements from such leaders as Henry Stanton, Theodore Parker, and William H. Brisbane.

Bailey's moderate approach with the *National Era* proved to be successful. By the end of its first year, the newspaper was publishing 11,000 copies a week, although many were given away. The great majority of the paper's circulation was in the North, but it was also exchanged with more than fifty newspapers in the South. The success of the *National Era* even led to the establishment in 1850 of the proslavery *Southern Press* in Washington. The *Press* claimed that the *National Era,* despite its seemingly moderate approach, was "clearly incendiary" because it opposed slavery and encouraged slaves to escape.[9]

By 1850 the *National Era* had a circulation of 15,000, and three years later it peaked at 28,000, making it the most widely read abolitionist publication and one of the largest-selling newspapers in the country. Bailey worked hard to make the *National Era* attractive and interesting. He used the best paper and type and made sure the layout was sharp and the articles well-edited. The editor, in turn, was enjoying his growing personal wealth. In 1851 he purchased a fine house on C Street and later a coach and horses. He and his wife enjoyed entertaining abolitionist leaders at their home. As the newspaper prospered, the gatherings became increasingly lavish affairs.[10]

The *National Era* certainly had its critics in the abolitionist community who were suspicious of Bailey's moderate approach—and undoubtedly at least a little jealous of his success. The *Anti-Slavery Bugle* sneered that the tone of the paper was "exceedingly judicious" and said it would never be "indicted for incendiarism [or] fanaticism." William Lloyd Garrison maintained that "a genuine anti-slavery journal would not be tolerated twenty four hours" in the capital. At its 1847 convention, the American Anti-Slavery Society denounced Bailey as a hopeless compromiser. Bailey staunchly defended the *National Era*'s approach, saying, "We take our stand as far South as we can, and appeal to the Southern people as men of like passions with ourselves." He noted caustically that his critics spoke from the relative safety of the North and he derided them as "impractical." He particularly singled out Garrison, calling him a "Self-Righteous Reformer" who never hesitated "to misrepresent and caricature an adversary." In the kind of venomous language Garrison regularly used, Bailey said the *Liberator*'s editor abhorred violence but "with a tongue set on fire by hell, scathes and devours what ever crosses his path."[11]

The success of the *National Era* certainly had an impact on the *Emancipator,* which had been the Liberty Party's most important press supporter. In early 1847 Joseph C. Lovejoy, brother of the martyred editor, became coeditor of the *Emancipator.* Later that year, Leavitt resigned from the paper he had been editing for the past ten years. Leavitt eventually joined the staff of a new Congregationalist publication, the *Independent.*[12]

For some the presence of an antislavery paper in the capital, even a generally moderate one, was too much, and the *National Era* eventually became the target of violence. In April 1848, two white men tried to help more than seventy Washington slaves escape down the Potomac River on the schooner *Pearl.* The slaves and their leaders were caught, but the incident sparked three days of violence in the city aimed at the *National Era.* The evening after the captured slaves were marched through the city to jail, a crowd broke the newspaper's windows and damaged its sign. On the advice of Seaton, who was also the mayor, Bailey issued a handbill denying any involvement with the escape attempt. He argued that he had published his antislavery newspaper with moderation and had "used but not abused" the right to publish freely. However, that did not stop the mob from returning and once again trying to break into the newspaper's office. Friends rushed to Bailey's home and escorted his family to the mayor's house for safety. Frustrated at their inability to seriously damage the *National Era,* a large crowd returned for a third time, but this time they were met by city authorities. The mob then went to Bailey's home determined to tar and feather him. The editor met the protesters outside and appealed to their sense of justice. They disbanded peacefully and did not threaten Bailey or the newspaper again.[13]

One of the reasons for starting the *National Era* was the belief that the time had come for a national dialogue on the issue of slavery's future. Texas had put the issue in the spotlight. Although Texas was not a part of the United States, that did not prevent Americans from settling there beginning in the 1820s. The vast region was suited to plantations and slave labor, but the Mexican government ended slavery in 1829. Worried Southern leaders saw Texas as a barrier to the westward expansion of slavery. Texans managed to get a special exemption to the ban on slavery from the Mexican government but never felt secure about it. When Mexico began to centralize its government, Texans revolted and the Republic of Texas was born in 1836. Talk of Texas joining the Union soon began, but many in the North feared increasing the South's already considerable political influence by adding the enormous slaveholding region to the country.

The annexation of Texas was the overriding subject during the election of 1844, in which Democrat James K. Polk defeated

Whig Henry Clay. Soon after the election, a joint resolution adding the new territory to the Union was approved by Congress, and three days before he left office President John Tyler signed the legislation. Texas had long claimed the Rio Grande River as its border with Mexico. Mexico, which had never recognized the independence of Texas, claimed a different border. Fighting erupted over the border dispute in early 1846, and in May President Polk declared war against Mexico.[14]

Abolitionist editors maintained that the Texas issue was clear evidence of the slave power conspiracy. They claimed that Southern leaders intended to force slavery into territories previously free in order to strengthen the institution and add new slave states to the Union. Garrison called the annexation a "crime unsurpassed in the annals of human depravity!" and added, "The Slave Power now holds a mastery over this nation, seemingly omnipotent." Although some in Congress conceded that slavery was unlikely to be popular in the west, others wanted to be sure. During debate on an 1846 appropriation bill for the war, Representative David Wilmot of Pennsylvania moved for an amendment that would prevent slavery from going into any territory acquired from Mexico. The Wilmot Proviso, as it came to be known, never received full congressional approval, but it sparked furious debate. The *Anti-Slavery Bugle* blasted Northern congressmen who did not support the measure. "There is no telling . . . what the craven-hearted dough-faces of the North will not do," the newspaper thundered. "The negro slave of the South is sold . . . their price to be paid in Southern favor and political preferment."[15]

War fever spread quickly, and American victories at Palo Alto and Resaca de la Palma heightened the convictions of continental destiny. However, abolitionists roundly denounced "Mr. Polk's War." Garrison announced with no apologies that he supported Mexico instead of the United States. He condemned as "diabolical" the popular motto, "My country, right or wrong," that frequently was used to disarm critics of American aggression. Writing in the *Emancipator,* Leavitt declared the war to be "a crime against the world" and branded the killing of Mexicans as "murder." The Mexican people were entirely justified, he wrote, "to cause every American now in arms in that Republic to be baptized in his own blood, either on the battle field in open conflict, or by private assassination by the road side or under cover of the night." Before he left Cincinnati, Bailey criticized the war in language so strong that he received new threats of violence and the mayor warned him that the city would not be able to protect him. Writing in the *National Era,* Whittier summed up the war as "a hideous joke—a grim farce, the plot of which must have been borrowed from beneath."[16]

After a series of victories over an outmatched Mexican Army, U.S. forces captured Mexico City in 1847. The Treaty of Guadalupe Hidalgo in March 1848 recognized the Rio Grande boundary of Texas. It also ceded to the United States the vast territory that would eventually become the states of California, Nevada, and Utah, most of New Mexico and Arizona, and parts of Oklahoma, Colorado, and Wyoming. Although abolitionist editors viewed the Mexican War as a Southern land grab, they took heart that the controversial Wilmot Proviso had broken the long-standing alliance between Northern and Southern Democrats over the future of slavery. A consensus against the extension of slavery into the western territories appeared to be emerging in the North. To some editors, the breakup of the old political parties also was at hand—and that was certainly good news for the antislavery cause.

Throughout the 1840s free blacks continued trying to publish their own newspapers, but none proved to be truly successful. Typical of the difficulties black editors encountered was the experience of Willis A. Hodges. A successful grocer in New York's black community, Hodges decided to start a newspaper after he was mistreated by an editor with the *New York Sun*. Hodges had penned a reply to a *Sun* editorial criticizing a proposed amendment to the state constitution that would remove the property qualification imposed on black voters. A *Sun* editor refused to run the reply unless Hodges paid fifteen dollars to run it as an advertisement. When Hodges argued that the editor was "only giving one side of the case, and your paper says that it 'shines for all,'" the editor replied, "The Sun shines for all white men, not black men." The editor then told Hodges to "get up a paper of your own if you want to tell your side of the story."[17]

With the help of Thomas Van Rensselaer, a runaway slave who operated a restaurant in New York, Hodges launched the *Ram's Horn* on January 1, 1847. The newspaper's name was taken from Joshua 6:5, and Hodges declared in the first issue, "We hope, like Joshua of old, to blow the 'Ram's Horn' (once a week) until the walls of slavery and injustice fall." Hodges and Van Rensselaer sent the *Ram's Horn* to hundreds of abolitionists and sold subscriptions at gatherings of New York blacks. The *Liberator* praised the newspaper for its dedication to "the abolition of slavery and the elevation of the colored population."[18]

Little is known about the *Ram's Horn* because only a few scattered issues of the newspaper exist. Hodges urged free blacks to seek an education and avoid the "great evil" of alcohol. And the newspaper spoke out against slavery in strong terms. In an editorial entitled "Slaves of the South, Now Is Your Time," the paper urged slaves to stop working without pay. "Make up your mind to die, rather than bequeath a state of slavery to your posterity." The *Ram's Horn* apparently was published weekly until June and then appeared irregularly for another year, when it closed for good.[19]

A young black abolitionist lecturer took notice of the black-owned newspapers and, ignoring the difficulties encountered by people like Hodges, became determined to join the ranks of editors. Frederick Augustus Washington Bailey had been born into a Maryland slave family. When he was eight years old, he was sent to his master's relatives in Baltimore to serve as a houseboy, and later a laborer in the shipyard. Bailey was a headstrong and often disobedient youth. At one point, he was flogged once a week for six months in at attempt to break his independent streak. However, Bailey was also intelligent and ambitious. Living in Baltimore, he saw free blacks earning a living on their own and he wanted that. In 1838 he escaped from his master by using forged papers to take a train headed to New York. The young man eventually settled in New Bedford, Massachusetts. There he changed his name to Frederick Douglass, taking his last name from a character in a Sir Walter Scott poem and changing the spelling to the way it was done by prominent black families in Baltimore and Philadelphia. In New Bedford, Douglass learned that racial prejudice was not limited to the South, and he was forced to take only menial jobs. He also began attending meetings of the local abolitionist society and started reading the *Liberator*.[20]

While attending an abolitionist meeting in 1841, Douglass was called upon to speak. He had grown into an imposing man, six feet tall with broad shoulders. His skin was bronze-colored and he wore his hair long and neatly parted on the side. Uncomfortable before the crowd, Douglass nonetheless spoke movingly about his experiences as a slave. Afterward, a leader of the Massachusetts Anti-Slavery Society asked Douglass to become a full-time lecturer, and he signed on. With his commanding speaking style, Douglass impressed audiences. "As a speaker he has few equals . . ." said a writer for the *Herald of Freedom*. "He has wit, arguments, sarcasm, pathos—all that first rate men show in their master efforts."[21]

Like many abolitionist speakers, Douglass was treated roughly by some audiences. At one meeting in Indiana, another abolitionist lecturer was knocked down by the crowd. Douglass grabbed a club and ran to the platform. The mob wrested the club from Douglass and, amid shouts of "kill the nigger," beat him severely. Douglass occasionally appeared with Garrison at lectures, and the young man learned a great deal from the veteran editor. "I have often been asked where I got my education," Douglass remarked many years later. "I have answered, from Massachusetts Abolition University: Mr. Garrison, president."[22]

In 1845 Douglass wrote about his experiences as a slave in the *Narrative of the Life of Frederick Douglass*. The book received warm reviews—the *New York Tribune* called it "an excellent piece of writing . . . to be prized as a specimen of the powers of the black race"—and it quickly became a big-seller with reformist readers. However, friends feared for his safety because the book revealed his master's identity as well as his own, and Douglass arranged a trip to Great Britain to prevent any chance of being captured. There he could give lectures and promote the sale of his book. During his trip, Douglass started thinking about publishing an abolitionist newspaper. Friends in England had raised $2,000 to support his abolitionist activities, and Douglass believed he could use the funds to purchase a press and printing equipment. When he returned to America, Douglass told friends of his plans. Several abolitionist leaders, including Garrison, discouraged him, telling him that his talents lay in speaking, not editing. Publishing a newspaper was difficult, and another abolitionist publication was not needed. "The land is full of the wreck of such experiments," wrote Garrison. Douglass initially took the advice and accepted an offer to write a regular column for the *National Anti-Slavery Standard*.[23]

Douglass resumed the lecture circuit, this time going out with Garrison. During their travels, the two men repeatedly witnessed the racism that existed in the North. On a trip from Philadelphia to Harrisburg, Douglass tried to sit in the rear of the railroad car instead of the customary spot near the door. A drunken lawyer pulled Douglass out of his seat and threw him into the aisle. After dusting himself off, Douglass told the man that only the obvious fact he was no gentleman saved him from a duel. At Harrisburg, Garrison was permitted to speak, but as soon as Douglass rose, the crowd pelted him with rotten eggs, brickbats, and firecrackers.

During the tour, Douglass changed his mind and decided to go through with his plan to start an abolitionist newspaper. He believed that the example of an outstanding publication, owned and edited by a black man, would be "powerful evidence that the Negro was too much of a man to be held a chattel." He also cited the existence of other black-owned publications, such as the *Ram's Horn*, as evidence that he could "accomplish the good which I sought." Douglass announced his plans in the *Ram's Horn*, saying that the new publication would "attack slavery in all its forms and aspects; advocate Universal Emancipation; exact the standard of public morality; promote the moral and intellectual improvement of the colored people; and to hasten the day of freedom to our three million enslaved fellow-countrymen."[24]

Using the donations from his supporters in England, Douglass purchased a printing press and other supplies. He decided to publish the paper from Rochester, New York, instead of the Atlantic seaboard, so that it would not interfere with the circulation of other abolitionist papers. Lying across Lake Ontario from Canada, Rochester was also the last stop on the Underground Railroad, and many runaways had found freedom with help from the city's abolitionist supporters. Presumably, the city would be friendly to an abolitionist publication.[25]

The first issue of the *North Star* appeared on December 3, 1847, and in the lead editorial Douglass wrote that he had long wished to establish a newspaper "under the complete control and direction of the immediate victims of slavery and oppression." It only made sense, he wrote, that "the man who *suffered the wrong* is the man to demand redress—that the man STRUCK is the man to CRY OUT—and that he who has *endured the cruel pangs of Slavery* is the man to *advocate Liberty.*" Douglass dedicated the newspaper to the cause of emancipation and vowed to "assail the ramparts of Slavery and Prejudice." He extolled the cultural significance of the paper's name for the nation's blacks. "Of all the stars in this 'brave, old, overhanging sky,' *The North Star* is our choice," he wrote. "To thousands now free in the British dominions it has been the Star of Freedom. To millions, now in our boasted land of liberty, it is the *Star of Hope.*"[26]

The *North Star*'s slogan was "Right is of no Sex—Truth is of no Color—God is the father of us all, and we are all Brethren." Douglass pledged the newspaper would fearlessly advocate the rights of free blacks, including the right to vote. Without identifying them, he referred to issues that have "unhappily divided the friends of freedom." Douglass said the views he would express in the newspaper would be consistent with those he had been expressing as a lecturer. He continued to be a sharp critic of the American Colonization Society. He called its leaders the enemies of free blacks and said the society's "alluring wiles and fascinating blandishments, must be closely watched, and firmly guarded against."[27]

Like other black-owned newspapers, Douglass's paper preached the importance of education, temperance, and moral character in order that blacks could achieve equality with whites. "The elevation of a high standard of morality is an indispensable requisite for our advancement," he wrote. "We are living in a land, where on the side of the oppressor there is power, and every dereliction on our part is trumpeted forth as a giant offence." The editor regularly highlighted black achievements in the *North Star,* and he encouraged free blacks to use their God-given talents to be successful. At the same time, Douglass was staunchly critical of blacks who were indifferent to the abolitionist cause. "Everyone of us should be ashamed to consider himself free while his brother is a slave," he wrote. To leave the fight against slavery to whites was to rob freedom of its value for blacks. "For our part, we despise a freedom and equality obtained for us by others, and for which we have been unwilling to labor," Douglass declared.[28]

Douglass published the *North Star* with Martin R. Delany, who had just resigned as editor of the *Mystery,* a black-owned publication in Pittsburgh. The newspaper's office, located at 25 Buffalo Street in the Talman Building in Rochester, was a single room that contained the editor's desk, type cases, mailing table, and a hand press. Two white apprentices, along with the

Douglass children, assisted with the various tasks to get the weekly paper out: setting the type and locking the forms, as well as folding and wrapping the papers for mailing.

Douglass was a talented writer with a clear and forceful editorial style. He relished the chance to speak out week after week on the issues of the day. And he took pride in the opportunity it provided him for his own intellectual development. Douglass frequently referred to his own experiences as a slave, and on the tenth anniversary of his escape from slavery, he used the *North Star* to publish an open letter to his old master, Thomas Auld. "Sir," began the letter, "The long and intimate, though by no means friendly relations which unhappily subsisted between you and myself, leads me to hope that you will easily account for the great liberty which I now take in addressing you in this open and public manner." With understandable pride, Douglass boasted in the letter of his accomplishments since escaping from Auld. He described the happy domestic life he enjoyed with his wife and four children. But he also expressed his bitterness at the "stripes on my back inflicted at your direction" and the way he was "dragged at the pistol's mouth" to be sold after a previous attempt to escape. (Douglass was never sold by Auld.) He asked what had become of his three sisters and a brother still owned by Auld, as well as a beloved grandmother who he claimed had been badly mistreated. Douglass told Auld that in his travels he had "made you the topic of conversation— thus giving you all the notoriety I could." And he promised to continue making use of Auld "as a weapon with which to assail the system of slavery—as a means of concentrating public attention on the system." However, Douglass insisted he had no personal animosity toward his former master. The editor closed the remarkable letter with words that would become among his best-remembered: "I am your fellow man, but not your slave."[29]

It did not take long for Douglass to learn that publishing an abolitionist journal was going to be a financial struggle—even for a widely known abolitionist. By the beginning of 1848, the editor was complaining about the small number of cash subscriptions. Expenses were running $55 a week, and without that much coming in, Douglass was forced to raise money by giving lectures "to keep our heads above water." By mid-1848, Douglass printed an urgent appeal for subscribers, saying that he had been forced to mortgage his home and, as a result, was "heavily in debt."[30]

The annexation of Texas, the Mexican War, and the Wilmot Proviso intensified the sectional debate within the Democratic and Whig parties. The situation also seemed to bode well for the Liberty Party's future, although it was not clear the party could take advantage of these developments. The election of 1848 provided plenty for the abolitionist press to write about as liberal Democrats and Whigs became increasingly disenchanted with their parties' stances on the slavery issue. Abolitionist papers reported the Barnburners walking out of the New York State Democratic convention. They also reported when so-called Conscience Whigs opposed the candidacy of Mexican War hero Zachary Taylor.

Then a coalition of Barnburners and Conscience Whigs—along with remnants of the Liberty Party—founded the Free Soil Party. Proclaiming their motto to be "free soil, free speech, free labor, free men," the party was not strictly abolitionist like the Liberty Party. However, the Free Soil platform called for an end to slavery in the District of Columbia. It also declared that slavery was a state rather than a national institution and, as such, must be excluded from the territories. Thousands of supporters met in Buffalo, New York. After endless speeches damning the slave power, the delegates nominated Martin Van Buren as their candidate for president.[31]

Douglass was one of several "colored gentlemen" who attended the Buffalo convention. He praised the party as arising "legitimately out of the principles which the American Anti-Slavery Society and the Liberty party have long been proclaiming." Although the new party was not all Douglass hoped for, he believed it was "a noble step in the right direction." Douglass was true to his word as the *North Star* supported Van Buren, even against the Liberty Party's candidate. The *Emancipator* also tried to rally Liberty loyalists to the Free Soil movement by declaring it "nothing less than the organization of the Liberty Party." Garrison found the party's platform generally weak, and, while he gave Free Soilers due credit for taking a tougher stance than others, he would not go so far as to give them his support. He also urged loyal abolitionists to "not lose sight of the true issue."[32]

Among those cheering for the Free Soil Party was a new abolitionist newspaper, the *Pittsburgh Saturday Visiter.* The weekly was founded by Jane Grey Swisshelm, an outspoken Pittsburgh native who was horrified at witnessing slavery while she lived in Kentucky for several years. After returning to her hometown, Swisshelm wrote for the *Spirit of Liberty* and the *Albatross,* two short-lived abolitionist publications in Pittsburgh. When the *Albatross* folded, Liberty Party leaders encouraged Swisshelm to start a newspaper. Using her inheritance to underwrite the venture, she launched the *Visiter* on December 20, 1847. The paper's name came from a verse in the book of Jeremiah: "Shall

I not visit for these things, saith the Lord, and shall not my soul be avenged on such a nation as this?"[33]

The *Visiter* attracted attention as much for the novelty of a woman editing a newspaper as for her views on slavery and other subjects. Swisshelm supported women's rights, including suffrage and the right to own property. But she argued that abolitionism and women's rights should remain separate issues because mixing them would only weaken both. "The women of this glorious Republic are sufficiently oppressed without linking their cause to that of the slave," she wrote. "The slave is sufficiently oppressed without binding him to the stake which has ever held woman in a state of bondage. There is no kind of reason why the American prejudice against color should be invoked to sink woman into a lower degradation than that she already enjoys—no kind of reason why the car of emancipation, for the slave, should have been clogged by tying to its wheels the most unpopular reform that ever was broached, by having all the women in the world fastened to the axle as a drag."[34]

When the Free Soil Party was founded, Swisshelm could not contain her enthusiasm. She told her readers that those who espoused the cause of freedom had a "sacred duty" to support the party's candidates in order to end slavery. Freedom required readers to vote for "FREE TERRITORY, FREE STATES, FREE LABOR, FREE MEN."[35]

Abolitionist editors recognized that a presidential victory was out of the question in 1848, but they hoped that a sizable Free Soil vote would show Congress that a compromise supporting slavery in the western territories would not be tolerated. They also hoped that a strong showing might lay the groundwork for an antislavery victory in 1852. But the election results were in no way encouraging. Whig candidate Taylor, a Louisiana slaveholder, won the election. The Free Soil candidate, Van Buren, did not carry a single state, and more than half his votes came from New York and Massachusetts. Moreover, only nine Free Soilers were sent to Congress. Despite the dismal showing, Bailey expressed optimism that Free Soil views on slavery had been inculcated in both major parties. However, Douglass was angry that Free Soilers had abandoned any united, national action against slavery. In an editorial entitled "What Has the Free Soil Movement Done?" he wrote that the party had promised a great deal, but accomplished little. In the end, it had proved to be simply "a dull and indolent concern."[36]

For his part, Garrison thanked God that the election was over because it was a political struggle that the abolitionists had managed to survive. "The people must be cured of this madness of politics, or their damnation is sure," he wrote in the *Liberator*. "Men, claiming to be moral and upright . . . must be driven from the polls as they are from the grog-shop and the house of ill-fame, by conviction of sin, by the power of conscience, by the potency of truth." He declared the Constitution to be "an evil instrument, to be regarded with abhorrence by all good men. The Union, erected as it is on the prostrated bodies of three millions of the people, deserves to be held in eternal execration, and dashed in pieces like a potter's vessel." In another editorial, Garrison found it unbelievable that abolitionists could support a party "disposed to maintain all the pro-slavery compromises of the Constitution." For abolitionists to "merge their principles" with the Free Soil Party was "the basest treachery." "No compromise, no partnership with slavery!" the editor wrote.[37]

By the time a new Congress convened at the end of 1849, it was clear that the issue of what to do with the new lands gained from Mexico was turning into a full-scale national crisis. Even though the Wilmot Proviso never passed the full Congress, it garnered enough support to alarm many Southern leaders. The careful sectional balance between free and slave states was tipping in a way they did not like, because California and other new territories were poised to join the free column. Alarmed about the future of the slave system, some Southern states began seriously talking about leaving the Union. Worried congressional leaders cast about furiously for a compromise that would keep the country together.[38]

Writing in the *North Star,* Douglass said the debate showed "to the entire nation and the world the real relation of this government and people to the slave system." Garrison did not take seriously the argument that compromise was needed because the United States was in danger of splitting. He declared that Northern sympathizers with slavery were "attempting to play the same old game, under a new phrase and for a new object." He argued that "the idol that is not to be worshipped is the AMERICAN UNION: and whoso falls not down before it, and gives not it his homage, is to be held up to popular execration."[39]

For his part, Bailey claimed that any compromise "fatal to liberty" was worse than dissolution of the Union. A union that perpetuated republican institutions was priceless, but a union that perpetuated slavery was a "crime and a curse." Bailey argued that a minority of Southerners in Congress was using parliamentary tactics to block the admission of California as a free state. "For ourselves, we have no hesitation in saying, that if this policy of Obstruction . . . is to become a usage whenever any question involving sectional considerations is concerned, the sooner the different sections of the country dissolve federal connection with each other the better for all," he wrote. "Union is worth nothing, if one interest is to possess a veto on all other interests—if the minority is to be suffered to impose an absolute check upon the majority."[40]

As Henry Clay's compromise moved through Congress early in 1850, Bailey argued that its passage would not stop the controversy over slavery. He said the abolitionist movement would not end because its advocates were opposed to the institution itself, not just its expansion. When Senator Daniel Webster, a longtime opponent of slavery and an influential member of Congress, surprisingly endorsed the compromise in a remarkable three-hour speech, abolitionists were stunned. A furious Bailey declared that the senator had abandoned his antislavery principles for political expediency. Two months later, the *National Era* published Whittier's bitter condemnation of Webster, the stirring poem "Ichabod." Garrison called Webster's speech "treachery to the cause of Liberty." For weeks, he republished denunciations of the senator from a host of people, including several poems by a young Walt Whitman, one of which compared Webster to the biblical Judas.[41]

Editors were hopeful that even if the compromise was passed by Congress, President Taylor would veto the measure. Up until that time, Taylor had opposed all compromise legislation. He insisted that California be admitted as a free state, while all other questions about slavery be postponed. When Taylor died suddenly in July 1850, the *National Era* declared it "a great calamity." With new president Millard Fillmore's support, Senator Stephen A. Douglas of Illinois guided the separate compromise measures through Congress.

The controversial Compromise of 1850 admitted California into the Union as a free state, while the status of New Mexico and Utah would be decided later. It banned public slave trading in the District of Columbia but still permitted slave ownership in the nation's capital. Even more appalling to slavery opponents, the compromise created the tough new Fugitive Slave Law, which empowered federal marshals to deputize bystanders to assist in seizing runaway slaves and permitted the cases of runaway slaves to be settled without jury trials.[42]

With a national crisis seemingly averted, Washington celebrated the Compromise of 1850. But while many hailed it as a solution to the slavery problem, abolitionist editors quickly rejected that view. For Bailey, the compromise did not deal with the issue of slavery itself. "The public mind of the North for the time is lulled. Wearied with the struggle, it is willing to rest, in the hope that Freedom may be the gainer from the settlement of the question in controversy," he wrote in the *National Era*. "But the quiet is transient . . . Between the antagonistic elements of Freedom and Slavery, a hollow truce may be occasionally patched up by adroit politicians, but there can be no solid, permanent peace." As the contentious new law was enforced against runaway slaves, the criticism grew even louder. Meanwhile, a fictional account of a runaway slave and his family, serialized in the pages of the *National Era,* riveted the country's attention to the issue like nothing had done before.[43]

SIX

THE MAINSTREAM PRESS
JOINS THE STRUGGLE

In the midst of the debate over the Compromise of 1850, a new piece of fiction appeared on the front page of the *National Era*. Written by abolitionist Harriet Beecher Stowe and entitled "Life Among the Lowly," it was the first installment in a series that told the fictional story of Tom, a slave torn from his family and sold by his owner. Since founding the *National Era,* Gamaliel Bailey had shown an eye for talented writers whose work would attract readers to the newspaper. All antislavery publications published fiction and poetry. However, Bailey seemed to get many of the best writers, and the newspaper published works by Nathaniel Hawthorne, William Cullen Bryant, Grace Greenwood, and others.

Still, the success of Stowe's story, which ran in the *National Era* for some forty weeks, far surpassed any series ever published in an abolitionist publication. Readers could not wait to read the next installment in the melodramatic story about the impact of slavery on blacks and whites. Stowe drew upon her keen observations of slavery in Kentucky and her experiences with runaway slaves in Cincinnati to create unforgettable characters such as Tom, Eliza, and Simon Legree. Later published under the title *Uncle Tom's Cabin,* the novel became the literary sensation of the era. It sold more than 10,000 copies in the first few weeks after publication and an astounding 300,000 copies in the first year alone. By the end of the decade, more than two million copies had been purchased in the United States. None other than Henry Wadsworth Longfellow said of the novel, "Never was there such a literary *coup-de-main* as this."[1]

Uncle Tom's Cabin was the most successful but certainly not the only way that abolitionist newspapers expressed outrage at the Fugitive Slave Law, part of the controversial Compromise of 1850. The story's publication ushered in a tumultuous decade, one in which abolitionist newspapers continued to call for an end to slavery—even as the country was increasingly splitting apart. The fighting among the antislavery press continued during the decade, most notably with a bitter feud between two of its best-known editors. Antislavery newspapers also continued to struggle financially. The difficulties were compounded by the fact that more of the country's mainstream press began supporting the abolitionist cause, thus making antislavery publications less unusual and less popular. The arguments of the abolitionist editors were strengthened as they linked the antislavery cause with the preservation of civil liberties.

For the abolitionist press, the Fugitive Slave Law was the most detestable feature of the Compromise of 1850. Editors had been working on behalf of runaway slaves for years before passage of the law, publicizing their plight with concrete examples of the evils of slavery. Publications regularly carried stories about runaways and the abolitionists who helped the fugitives escape.

Abolitionist leaders recognized, as Russel B. Nye has written, that "a single runaway, taken in a Northern town by a Southern sheriff, could do more to excite antislavery feelings than a dozen societies; his capture gave concrete illustration of those evils of slavery long preached in the abstract."[2]

One of the most widely publicized early cases in the abolitionist press was Captain Jonathan Walker, who was arrested in 1844 for helping slaves to escape to the Bahamas. He was convicted and fined, and the letters "SS" for "slave stealer" were branded on his right hand. Abolitionist newspapers devoted extensive space to Walker's trial and captivity. That same year, Charles T. Torrey, a theological student and member of the Massachusetts Anti-Slavery Society, was arrested in Baltimore for helping a slave escape. He was convicted and sentenced to prison, where he developed tuberculosis. As he was dying in jail, Torrey wrote letters to his friends, and the letters received wide coverage in antislavery newspapers.[3]

But the abolitionist press waged outright war against the Fugitive Slave Law. The *Pennsylvania Freeman* called it "the most atrocious law which has ever gained the sanction of the United States Congress . . . it fixes a blot of infamy upon the character of that body which . . . all the billows of Time can never wash away." Editors claimed the law endangered not only escaped slaves but also free blacks, who were legal citizens in most Northern states. They published cases of free blacks who were seized and taken to the South, including some in their own communities. They also warned that it was only a matter of time before whites would see their rights similarly denied. "The Fugitive Slave Law will be made to look small by the side of the next encroachment upon the Rights of Man," argued William Lloyd Garrison in a speech that was widely reprinted.[4]

Although most editors had traditionally preached nonviolence, the law changed many minds. "The only way to make the Fugitive Slave Law a dead letter is to make half a dozen or more dead kidnappers," Douglass proclaimed. Editors noted with satisfaction the angry reaction to the law by communities in the North. If the goal of the bill's supporters had been to "create deep excitement in the free states, to extend agitation on the subject of slavery, to provoke into intense activity every latent feeling against their peculiar system . . . they could not have devised a more effectual method," said the *National Era*. "The excitement occasioned by the passage of the Fugitive Slave Law is becoming more intense with every hour," wrote Oliver Johnson in the *Anti-Slavery Bugle*. "The papers are filled with discussions of the subject and with the proceedings of meetings held to denounce the law. We cannot pretend to notice one in fifty of these assemblages."[5]

In reporting and editorializing on the law, the abolitionist press appealed to the humanitarian sympathies of readers. Newspapers were filled with lurid accounts of the suffering and treatment of fugitive blacks. The *Anti-Slavery Standard* ran a weekly column called "The Hunt," and the *Anti-Slavery Bugle* averaged three reports of fugitive slaves a week. Passage of the law renewed the interest of some in colonization, but most abolitionist editors still had nothing but contempt for the plan. "Of all the impudent, soulless organizations that ever existed, the American Colonization is entitled to rank as first," declared the *Anti-Slavery Bugle*. "Under the guise of philanthropy, under the pretence of benefiting the Afro-American it assumes the right to send him from the land of his nativity; and in order to obtain the means to effect his expatriation appeals to the worst prejudices of the whites, fosters their hatred of the colored man, and pronounces his degradation here inevitable, his oppression irremediable."[6]

The Fugitive Slave Law spurred the popularity of the Underground Railroad as a means of helping slaves to escape into Canada. The three main "lines" ran from Missouri northeast across Illinois, from Kentucky and Virginia across Ohio and western Pennsylvania, and from Maryland and Virginia across eastern Pennsylvania. By 1851, promoters boasted that a slave could be run from any border state to Canada in forty-eight hours. No trustworthy figures are available about the number of slaves who escaped to freedom using the Underground Railroad, but most now believe that it is far fewer than either abolitionists or slave owners claimed. Still, the abolitionist press widely publicized the railroad, describing heroic stories of runaway slaves and their "conductors." Douglass was one of the leaders of the Underground Railroad in Rochester. One of his newspaper employees said it was not unusual for Douglass to find a fugitive on the steps of the office when he arrived in the morning. During one two-week period in 1854, the editor told readers that he had helped more than thirty runaways escape into Canada.[7]

The antislavery press also seized upon several high-profile runaway cases for their propaganda value. During the "Jerry Rescue" in 1851, a group of abolitionists broke into the jail in Syracuse, New York, rescued runaway Jerry McHenry, and took him to Canada. The rescuers were arrested but later released. Thereafter they held an annual anniversary meeting in Syracuse to celebrate their act of defiance. The "Battle of Christiana" provided even more sensational headlines for the abolitionist press. Christiana, Pennsylvania, was a Quaker community that welcomed fugitive slaves. On September 11, 1851, a Maryland slave owner, accompanied by relatives and three deputy marshals, came to the town looking for two escaped slaves reported to be hiding in the home of a black man. They soon found the fugitives, who were being protected by armed men. A gun battle ensued during which the slave owner and three blacks were killed. Garrison staunchly defended the Christiana fugitives. "A man hunted for his liberty has a *right to fight* to the last drop of blood, and we honor him," the editor wrote. When a federal grand jury indicted thirty-six blacks and five whites on charges of treason in connection with the killings, Bailey dared the government to pursue the case. "Should you really be able to accomplish such a miracle of infamy, you will arouse a story which will whelm you and your aiders and abetters in infamy," he warned. "Hang men for constructive high treason, and you will have civil war, unless American citizens are bastard sons of 1776." In the end, Bailey and others could rejoice. When it became clear that a sympathetic jury was not going to convict the men for treason, the government dropped the charges.[8]

But perhaps no case received so much attention as that of Anthony Burns, a slave preacher who escaped to Boston. In 1854 Burns was caught, jailed, and claimed by his owner. Abolitionists held a public meeting to protest the jailing, and afterward a group of men stormed the jail and freed Burns, but they killed a marshal in the process. A Massachusetts court ordered that Burns be returned to his owner. As thousands of antislavery supporters in the city jeered, armed federal troops escorted Burns to a ship waiting to take him back to Virginia. The *Liberator* declared that the decision sending Burns back to slavery made the Declaration of Independence "a lie" and the Golden Rule "an absurdity." The *National Era* warned that if the federal government continued to enforce such an unpopular law, it would become "a stench in the nostrils of the People."[9]

Garrison put the final touch to the incident at the Massachusetts Anti-Slavery Society's annual Fourth of July picnic. More than 600 abolitionists gathered in a grove of oaks near the town of Framingham, sixteen miles outside of Boston, for the event. The speaker's platform was festooned with two white flags labeled Kansas and Nebraska, and an American flag was edged with black crepe. Among the speakers were such antislavery luminaries as Sojourner Truth, Wendell Phillips, Lucy Stone, and Henry David Thoreau. Then it was Garrison's turn to speak. After giving a gloomy recasting of his familiar themes, Garrison held up a copy of the Fugitive Slave Law, struck a match, and set the document on fire. He did the same thing with a copy of the decision in the Burns case. Then Garrison held up a copy of the U.S. Constitution, struck another match, and in dramatic fashion burned the "covenant with death," as he had called the document so many times. "So perish all compromises with tyranny," the editor thundered.[10]

For the abolitionist press, the Fugitive Slave Law was simply more proof of the threat that the slave power posed to the country. Slave owners and their supporters had been condemned by antislavery editors for decades. Writing in 1837, James G. Birney had called slave supporters "a Despotism which has attempted to fetter the free mind of the North." However, after the Compromise of 1850, the slave power became the primary focus of abolitionist attacks. A writer for the *Anti-Slavery Bugle* argued that "the slave power has already seized upon the General Government, and has overthrown the rights of the free States, and made the citizens slave citizens . . . The struggle between the slave and the free institutions is for existence. They are antagonistic principles and cannot exist long together—one or the other must fall."[11]

Bailey, in particular, hammered home the theme in editorials with titles such as "Despotism," "The Privileged Class," and "A Dark Conspiracy." "It is not negro slavery alone from which the slave states need deliverance," he argued in the *National Era*. "First, the whites must regain their lost rights—and then there may be a chance for the negroes." Editors also argued that the slave power conspiracy increasingly included Northern commercial interests that wanted to see slavery grow. The *Anti-Slavery Bugle* proclaimed that "the wealth of the North, and the wealth of the South are combined to crush the liberal, free, progressive spirit of the age."[12]

At the same time the abolitionist press was railing against the slave power, the South was repeatedly playing into the hands of its critics. In several states, slaveholding minorities sought to reopen the slave trade. Antislavery editors seized upon the proposals as evidence that the slave power was trying to entrench itself even more. Newspapers kept count of Southern requests to reopen the slave trade and warned Congress of the dire consequences of repealing the ban on it.[13]

In using the threat of the slave power as a propaganda device, abolitionist editors also exploited the belief of some that what slave owners eventually wanted to do was to enslave whites, particularly poor and immigrant groups. Antislavery papers gleefully reprinted references to such practices made by Southern politicians and editors. The *Anti-Slavery Bugle* reprinted how the *Richmond Examiner* had pointed out that in biblical times slaves were not blacks and that "confining the jurisdiction of slavery to that race would be to weaken its scriptural authority . . . Slavery black or white is necessary." Editors aimed this message particularly at immigrants who, because of their status, felt particularly threatened. Immigrants, the editors argued, must support the abolitionist cause or someday their children might become slaves. The *Anti-Slavery Bugle* asked, "What security have the Germans and the Irish that their children will not, within a hundred years, be reduced to slavery in this land of their adoption?"[14]

In the midst of the controversy over the Fugitive Slave Law, differences between Douglass and Garrison degenerated into a slanderous personal feud that sullied the names of both editors. The problems began in 1851 when Douglass moved to save the struggling *North Star* by merging it with the *Liberty Party Paper* to form a new weekly, *Frederick Douglass' Paper*. Despite the wide respect in which Douglass was held, the *North Star* had never enjoyed a large circulation. Douglass had even considered closing the newspaper several times but always changed his mind. On June 30, 1851, the first issue of *Frederick Douglass' Paper* appeared bearing the motto, "All Rights for All."

Gerrit Smith, a major supporter of the Liberty Party, had courted Douglass for months. Smith had subscribed to the *North Star* since its founding and made periodic contributions to the newspaper. Some Garrisonians, who still considered Douglass disloyal for starting his own publication, believed the editor to be little more than a Smith sycophant. Smith agreed to take over the debts of the *North Star* and provide financial support for the new publication. The name change was made, Douglass maintained, to distinguish the weekly "from the many papers with 'Stars' in their titles." But undoubtedly he and Smith also believed that the use of his well-known name would attract more subscribers.[15]

Garrison, who had long feared that Douglass might become captive to "Liberty Party thinking," nonetheless was hurt by his colleague's change in thinking. He maintained that the name change was egotistical and said the new name lacked the strong cultural associations of the *North Star* or *Ram's Horn*. A bitter editorial war soon ensued between the two antislavery giants. Never one to bite his tongue, Garrison said he wished that Douglass's new journal had a real title instead of just his name. Douglass immediately fired back, saying that he saw no more incongruity in naming the paper after himself than "we do in calling a certain book, which we value very highly, Garrison's Thoughts on Colonization."[16]

Later, when Douglass proposed the creation of a National Black Council and a manual training school for blacks, he was criticized by Garrisonians for the racial exclusivity of these proposals. Douglass took the censure personally, charged that the *Liberator*'s editor was behind it, and said that Americans showed little concern for the welfare of blacks. Garrison claimed that Douglass had ostracized himself and called him an "unscrupulous schismatic." He said Douglass believed the color of his skin would shield him from critics. He also admonished Douglass not to criticize those "who had been his best friends and to whom he is eternally indebted for his emerging from obscurity." Friends of both men, including Stowe, urged them to end the fighting for the good of the antislavery cause. The two editors eventually called a truce, but the wounds festered for years.[17]

Although supporters had hoped the Compromise of 1850 would end the dispute over slavery's future, that hope was clearly in vain. Pressures were accelerating to open the remainder of the Louisiana Purchase territory to settlement. At midcentury, the United States was in the midst of an economic boom financed by the discovery of gold in California and massive exports of cotton. The strong economy made the country a magnet for immigrants, particularly from Ireland and Germany. Railroad lines were pushing south and west, and ambitious plans were underway for a transcontinental railroad. Senator Stephen A. Douglas, who had aspirations for the White House, wanted a northern route for any railroad running west to the Pacific coast. The Democrat moved to organize the vast region west of Iowa and Missouri as the Nebraska Territory. But because the territory lay north of the 36°30′ parallel, an area in which slavery had been prohibited by the Missouri Compromise of 1820, Douglas needed Southern support for his measure. Though Douglas knew it would create "a hell of a storm," he proposed creating two territories—Nebraska and Kansas—leaving the question of slavery for residents of those territories to decide and thus repealing the prohibition of slavery north of 36°30′.[18]

Furious abolitionist editors thundered against the "Kansas Plot," calling it yet another example of slave power treachery. Douglass said congressional leaders were "guilty of any amount of low scoundrelism" in seeking to "throw off the obligations of a bargain." The *Pennsylvania Freeman* urged readers "to flood Congress with petitions against this unholy scheme." The Kansas-Nebraska bill, Garrison wrote in the *Liberator,* was "against the laws of God and the rights of universal man—in subversion of plighted faith, in utter disregard of the score of the world, and for purposes as diabolical as can be conceived or summated here on earth."[19]

As the legislation was taking shape, Bailey launched a daily edition of the *National Era* on January 2, 1854, in an all-out effort to defeat the bill. The editor had considered starting a daily during the congressional debate in 1850 but was not in a financial position to do so. Now that the *National Era* was on more sound footing, he committed $5,000 to the daily and threw himself into the venture. Bailey warned that a vast territory would be "thrown open to Slavery, so that a cordon of slaveholding States may be drawn upon the Free West." Kill the legislation, he declared, "or it will give the Slave Power an ascendancy in this country, the terrible results of which no mind can fathom." Bailey also published a forceful appeal by Salmon P. Chase, William H. Seward, Charles Sumner, and other Democrats, known as the "Appeal of the Independent Democrats to the People of the United States." This masterful piece of antislavery propaganda warned of a "monstrous plot" to convert the free territories into a "dreary region of despotism, inhabited by masters and slaves." It was quickly reprinted by newspapers across the North.[20]

Despite the opposition, the Kansas–Nebraska bill passed and President Franklin Pierce signed it into law. The public exploded. Across the North, people condemned what they saw as a craven submission to Southern demands and the undoing of a historic compromise. Angry rallies and resolutions deplored what many called the "Nebraska Fraud." Even Douglas noted derisively, "I could travel from Boston to Chicago by the light of my own effigy."

As historians have pointed out, it would be wrong to suggest that the public anger was directed at the institution of slavery. Most of the criticism centered on what opponents believed was a growing Southern conspiracy to spread slavery into the free territories. Nonetheless, abolitionist editors suddenly found themselves speaking in the same voice as thousands of other Americans. And they were increasingly joined by mainstream publications which decried the threat posed by an aggressive "slavocracy." "Were it a bad measure, we might speak of it calmly and measuredly," wrote editor Horace Greeley in the

New York Tribune, "but as an act of deliberate bad faith, impelled by the most sordid motives and threatening the most calamitous results, we must treat it as we do other gigantic perfidies and crimes."[21]

The angry reaction to the Kansas-Nebraska Act gave radicals in the North the opportunity they had been looking for. Even before Congress passed the bill, former Whigs and Democrats, along with Free Soilers, joined forces to form what would become the Republican Party. The *National Era*'s Bailey played an important role in the party's creation. Bailey had been one of the first to call for a "Party of Freedom" to oppose the coalition of Whigs and Democrats that had worked to repeal the Missouri Compromise. The editor personally urged congressmen opposed to the Kansas-Nebraska Act to "forget their party differences" and "*unite,* Unite, UNITE!" Badgered by Bailey and others, some thirty members of the House of Representatives agreed that a new political organization was needed to check Southern aggression. Calling themselves at various times the Fusion, People's, and Independent party, members eventually settled on the name *Republican.*[22]

At the same time a rival had emerged, the Know-Nothing Party. Organized in 1849 as the Order of the Star-Spangled Banner, for years it was little more than a political pressure group. But by 1854, the party had become an influential group with strength in both the North and South. The Know-Nothings took a strong nativist stance with their antagonism toward immigrants, especially Irish Catholics. But what made it a real threat to Republicans was the party's moderate antislavery views.[23]

Bailey had nothing but contempt for the Know-Nothings, calling the party a "detestable organization" that was "repugnant to the doctrine of equal rights." "You have no more right to disenfranchise your brother man," he wrote, "than you have to disenfranchise your colored neighbor; nor, have you a right to make membership in any religious sect, a disqualification for office." Garrison mocked the party as "burrowing in secret like a mole in the dark" and criticized it for "proscribing men on account of their birth and peculiar religious faiths." Although the Know-Nothings scored a stunning victory when their candidate won the Massachusetts governorship and the party took control of the state legislature, Garrison dismissed this as little more than "temporary excitement."[24]

At the same time, abolitionist editors criticized Republicans for failing to speak out more forcefully against slavery. Douglass wrote, "Abolitionists can be induced to follow the Republican movement only under the teachings of a plausible and sinuous political philosophy, which is the grand corrupter of all reforms." He later described the party as "a heterogeneous mass of political antagonisms, gathered from defunct Whiggery, disaffected Democracy, and demented, defeated and disappointed Native Americanism."[25]

While the parties were considering platforms and candidates in spring 1856, violence was spreading in Kansas and Missouri. When a proslavery judge instructed a grand jury to indict members of the free-state government for treason, an armed band of Missourians used it as an excuse to storm Lawrence, Kansas, a bastion of the antislavery forces, on May 21. The band burned the governor's home and plundered various businesses, including the town's two antislavery newspapers, the *Herald of Freedom* and the *Kansas Free State*. The attack was promptly labeled the "Sack of Lawrence" by the antislavery and Republican press.[26]

Just days before the attack on Lawrence, Charles Sumner of Massachusetts had denounced "the Crime Against Kansas" on the floor of the Senate. He declared that "murderous robbers from Missouri" had committed a "rape of virgin territory, compelling it to the hateful embrace of slavery." In his diatribe, Sumner singled out Senator Andrew Butler of South Carolina for choosing as a mistress "the harlot, Slavery." The speech caused an uproar, and Congressman Preston Brooks, a cousin of Butler, believed he had to respond. On May 22 Brooks walked into the Senate chamber after adjournment and confronted Sumner, telling the senator that his speech was an outrageous libel on South Carolina and his relative. He then beat Sumner over the head repeatedly with a gold-headed cane. Sumner had to be hospitalized, and he did not return to the Senate for three years.[27]

Antislavery newspapers were horrified by the brutal assault on Sumner, as well as the view of many in the South that Brooks was a hero for defending the honor of Butler. Editors declared the attack to be entirely unprovoked and said the senator simply was arguing for what he believed to be right. "What is the Union good for," Bailey asked, "if the Representatives of the different States meet, as enemies, not to deliberate and freely confer on matters of common interest, but to defy each other to mortal combat?" The growing number of Republican newspapers joined in the criticism. The Albany *Evening Journal* declared that Brooks had "the voice and temper of an overseer" and said the caning meant that the "discipline of the Plantation has been introduced into the Senate." "Has it come to this?" asked the *New York Evening Post*. "Are we to be chastised as they chastise their slaves? Are we too, slaves, slaves for life; a target for their brutal blows, when we do not comport ourselves to please them?"[28]

The angry rhetoric continued in the months leading up to the 1856 presidential election between Democrat James Buchanan, Republican John C. Frémont, and Know-Nothing Millard Fillmore. During the campaign, the *National Era* was every bit a Republican organ. Bailey offered the newspaper at a special price. He repeatedly countered charges by Democrats and Know-Nothings that a Republican president would lead to the breakup of the Union. He said the choice was between Frémont, who would preserve freedom in the territories, and Buchanan, who would serve the interests of the slave power by permitting the creation of new slave states. He called Fillmore a "small neighborhood candidate" who was unable to attract wide support. Bailey also tried to turn the persistent rumors that Frémont was a Catholic to his advantage. "Pray heaven that this may be the last election in which a man's religious faith or connection may be brought into the question of his fitness for office," he wrote. "For one, whenever this subject is brought up, we must enter our stern protest against the anti-Christian, anti-American dogma of a miserable bigotry, that none but a Protestant is qualified for civil office."[29]

For months Douglass had refused to endorse the Republicans because they did not "give a full recognition to the humanity of the Negro." But in mid-August the editor changed his mind and threw his support to Frémont. Responding to critics who charged he was waffling, Douglass claimed he was not being inconsistent and said the switch was due to "a difference of Policy, not of Principle." Although the Republican Party did not go as far to end slavery as he would like, that was no reason to withhold his support. "A man was not justified in refusing to assist his fellow-men to accomplish a good thing simply because his fellows refuse to accomplish some other good thing which they deem impossible," he wrote. He maintained that Frémont would "not countenance slaveholding aggression."[30]

For his part, Garrison argued that "against Buchanan and Fillmore, it seems to us the sympathies and best wishes of every enlightened friend of freedom must be on the side of Fremont." The endorsement of a candidate by a man who had previously disdained politics signaled just how much Garrison's views had changed. Before then the editor had criticized the Republican Party's views on slavery as "partial, one-sided, geographical." But with the election looming, he wrote of the party that in "general intelligence, virtuous character, humane sentiment, and patriotic feeling—as well as in the object it is seeking to accomplish—it is incomparably better than the other rival parties; and its success, *as against those parties,* will be a cheering sign of the times."[31]

Bailey blamed the threats of disunion and the appeal of nativism for Frémont's loss to Buchanan in the election. He said Republicans had erred in not clearly distancing themselves from the Know-Nothings. To fight a pro-Southern Buchanan administration, Bailey called on Republicans to adopt "a bold, straight-forward, and honest course free from all entangling alliances, in rigid accordance with their own principles, unadulterated by contradicting elements."[32]

On March 6, 1857, just two days after Buchanan took the oath of office, a Supreme Court decision in the case of *Dred Scott v. Sandford* rocked the country once again. Scott was a former slave who sued for his freedom in 1846, arguing that he had become a free man when his owners took him to Illinois. A Missouri court ruled in favor of Scott, but the state supreme court overturned the ruling. When a federal court agreed with the ruling, Scott appealed to the U.S. Supreme Court. By a 7–2 vote, the justices denied Scott's suit asking for his freedom. Speaking for the majority that included five Southerners, Chief Justice Roger B. Taney also used the ruling to declare the Missouri Compromise unconstitutional, saying Congress had no right to exclude slavery from the territories. Taney went on to express the opinion that blacks had no constitutional rights of citizenship. Blacks were "so far inferior," he wrote, that they possessed no rights before the law that whites were "bound to respect."[33]

It was one of the most partisan judicial decisions in American history, and editors denounced the court's decision in blistering language. "It makes slavery the primary law of the Union," thundered the *Anti-Slavery Bugle,* "the sustaining and defending of human chattelism the main object of the Constitution." The *Independent,* a Congregationalist publication that was becoming increasingly forceful in its editorials against slavery, called the court's ruling the "moral assassination of a race" and declared that it "cannot be obeyed."[34]

Bailey, who helped raise money to pay the legal expenses of Scott, predicted that the decision opening all the territories to slavery would "hasten the great Revolution" and mean a Republican victory in the 1860 presidential election. "We beg the intelligent reader to consider for five minutes the character of the decision of the Supreme Court," wrote Sydney Gay in the *Anti-Slavery Standard.* "How it ignores all history; how it sets all law at defiance; how it outrages common sense; how it scorns human pretences; how it tramples upon the plainest principles of the Christian religion; how it laughs at liberty; how it scoffs at democracy; and how it scouts all Northern pretension to freedom of thought, or freedom of act, or freedom of conscience." Surprisingly, Garrison was generally silent about the ruling. He put excerpts from Taney's opinion in the *Liberator's*

"Refuge of Oppression" column and reprinted angry editorials from other Northern newspapers. But generally he let others rail against Taney and the Court.[35]

Among the most prominent critics of the Court's ruling were the growing number of mainstream Republican newspapers published across the North, many in major cities. In fact, more and more of the party's publications sounded like abolitionist newspapers in their sharp criticism of the South. The *Chicago Tribune* warned that the Court had taken a step toward "making slavery the law of the Republic." "Freedom has been declared unconstitutional," the *Milwaukee Free Democrat* said of the decision. And the *New York Tribune*'s Greeley wrote that "any slave-driving editor or Virginia bar-room politician could have taken the Chief Justice's place on the bench, and with the exception of a little bolder speaking up, nobody would have perceived the difference." Criticism of the ruling was so widespread that one correspondent remarked, "If epithets and denunciations could sink a judicial body, the Supreme Court of the United States would never be heard from again."[36]

Unquestionably, the most important Republican newspaper was Greeley's widely read *New York Tribune*. Founded as one of the first "penny" newspapers, the *Tribune* originally supported the Whigs. But Greeley embraced the views of the Republican party and over time became an opponent of slavery. "Uncle Horace," as he was known to many, had long admired the intellectual Sydney Gay, and in 1857 he lured him away from the *Anti-Slavery Standard* to the *Tribune*. Gay worked tirelessly to keep the *Tribune's* editorial page consistently antislavery, no small feat given Greeley's often erratic views. In 1862, Gay succeeded Charles A. Dana as managing editor, and under his direction the powerful *Tribune* attacked slavery with even more fervor.[37]

Although antislavery editors were glad to have the editorial company of the *Tribune* and other Republican journals, they could not compete with the financial resources of metropolitan dailies that employed large staffs and brimmed with advertising. The *National Era,* in particular, was hurt by the popularity of the cheap dailies. Its circulation began to decline, and in the fall Bailey appealed for help from antislavery readers. The newspaper was the "pioneer press of Liberty on Slave Soil," the editor wrote, and had established "the right of free discussion in Washington." Bailey claimed the journal had been hurt by Republicans who wanted it to "lose much of its prominence & influence." He said he would work for the abolitionist cause "until flesh and heart fail," but unless more readers subscribed, the *National Era* must cease publishing.[38]

Then suddenly Bailey's influential voice was lost. The 51-year-old editor, who had suffered from poor health for several years, booked a trip to Europe in the spring of 1859 in the hopes of resting and regaining his health. In the May 26 issue of the *National Era,* Bailey explained the reasons for his trip and promised to send letters back to the newspaper. But his condition worsened soon after the ship departed from New York. Bailey collapsed on June 5 and died soon afterward.[39]

Abolitionist editors—joined by their colleagues in the Republican press—eulogized Bailey's passing. John Greenleaf Whittier called Bailey's death "a public calamity." "He was one of those men who mould and shape the age in which they live," the poet wrote. Not surprisingly, the *Liberator* was more reserved in its praise. Although it called Bailey a man of "true courage" and "unquestioned integrity," his newspaper was "more distinguished for its literary merits than for its abolitionism." On the other hand, the *New York Evening Post* assigned

Bailey "no small degree" of credit for the growth of the political movement against slavery. It said the *National Era* "led the nucleus of the party—the stern, uncompromising Anti-Slavery men."[40]

As far back as the Nat Turner rebellion, abolitionist editors had debated what role violence should play in the antislavery struggle. In the fall of 1859, a wild-eyed abolitionist named John Brown put the issue before the nation. Brown was already well known in antislavery circles. In an essay for the *Ram's Horn*, he had argued that blacks were better off in resisting slavery than by "tamely submitting to every species of indignity." For years Brown helped fugitive slaves escape via the Underground Railroad and he befriended many black leaders, most notably Douglass. From 1855 to 1857, Brown fought against proslavery militia for control of the Kansas territory. He gained a reputation for courage during the guerilla fighting, but also a bad name when he led the "massacre" at Pottawatomie Creek in which five proslavery men were murdered.[41]

Brown had no use for abolitionists who only talked about ending slavery. What was needed was action, he believed. With the secret support of some abolitionist leaders, Brown spent months plotting an assault on the federal arsenal at Harpers Ferry, sixty miles northwest of Washington, D.C. He wanted to seize the arsenal's stockpile of weapons and arm nearby slaves with the hope of starting a massive revolt that would force the country to end slavery. On October 16, 1859, he and nineteen black and white followers briefly gained control of the arsenal, but the next day they were crushed by state and federal troops. Seventeen people were killed in the fighting, including ten raiders, two of whom were Brown's sons.[42]

The daring raid shocked the nation like few other events in its history. An outraged South, which had always worried about large-scale slave insurrections, called for Brown's blood. Many in the North considered Brown mad, but his eloquence in defending his actions during his trial and his courage during his execution, six weeks after the raid, changed opinions. The fanatical abolitionist had become a martyr. "Another Hero's name is written on the roll of History!" declared the *Anti-Slavery Standard*. "The homely name of John Brown is henceforward an immortal one and his memory safe among the priceless treasures of mankind."[43]

Garrison wrestled with the question of Brown's guilt. In his first editorial after the raid, he called the assault "well intended but sadly misguided." He accepted the sincerity of Brown's belief that he was "raised up by God to deliver the oppressed in this country, in the way he has chosen, as did Moses in relation to the deliverance of the captive Israelites." Garrison finally decided that sometimes violence was indeed necessary. The *Liberator* reprinted a speech he gave at a memorial meeting: "As a peace man—I am prepared to say: 'Success to every slave insurrection in the South.'"[44]

Brown's raid put the Republican press on the defensive. While insisting that they did not condone what the abolitionist had done, editors proclaimed it to be an understandable reaction to the crimes of slaveholders and the Democratic administration which refused to move against the institution. They predicted that insurrections would only stop when slavery was outlawed.[45]

Douglass challenged those who considered Brown to be insane for having attacked the arsenal. He argued instead that Brown was moved by compassion for the slaves. Moreover, his course of action was in keeping with the nature of slavery itself. "Slavery is a system of brute force," he wrote. "It shields itself behind might, rather than right. It must be met with its own weapons." Otherwise, Douglass was silent about Brown—and with good reason. The editor had first met Brown in 1848, at which time Brown discussed a plan to establish squads of armed men to help slaves to escape. Nothing came of the plan, but the two men maintained cordial, if infrequent, relations. After returning from Kansas, Brown began discussing a raid into Virginia. He stayed at the Douglass home on several occasions, but never revealed the details of his plan until the two men met again just weeks before the raid. Brown urged Douglass to take part, but the editor refused, saying any attack on the arsenal was suicidal. When Brown was captured, an alarmed Douglass feared he might be implicated by the authorities. At the urging of friends, he fled to Canada. Douglass had already been planning a trip to England before the raid. From Canada he sailed for England, where he stayed for several months until the furor subsided. He wrote an open letter to the readers of *Douglass' Monthly* saying that he was relinquishing his editorial duties to go on the long-planned tour. In the letter he only mentioned Brown in passing.[46]

When Douglass returned to the United States in 1860, he and other abolitionist editors were in the political mainstream. The extraordinary events of the past four years had given Republicans a genuine shot at the White House. The party was also helped by a sharply divided Democratic Party. For months before that party's convention, the Southern wing had been demanding a plank in the platform pledging a federal slave code for the territories. Members were threatening to walk out if party leaders refused. Charleston had been selected by Democrats to host the convention in the hope that the choice of a Southern city would promote unity. But it proved to be disastrous. When Northern delegates who supported the candidacy of Stephen Douglas pushed through a platform without the slave code, fifty members from the lower South bolted. Douglas could not muster the votes required for nomination, nor could anyone else. Dispirited members adjourned and agreed to meet six weeks later in Baltimore. There they managed to nominate Douglas, but the damage to the party had already been done. The bolters organized their own convention and nominated Vice President John C. Breckenridge of Kentucky on a platform supporting the slave code.

In editorial after editorial, abolitionist editors reveled in the controversy that was roiling the Democrats. However, they were not entirely sold on Abraham Lincoln, the Republican Party's unlikely nominee. To the surprise of many in the party, the one-term congressman from Illinois had bested several other better-known candidates, including abolitionist leader William H. Seward, to secure the Republican nod. The man known as Honest Abe was a moderate. He had declared in his 1858 debates with Stephen A. Douglas that "I have no purpose directly or indirectly to interfere with the institution of slavery in the States where it exists. I believe I have no lawful right to do so, and I have no inclination to do so." However, Lincoln had also called slavery "a moral, social, and political wrong." And in his memorable "A House Divided" speech, he argued that "this Government cannot endure, permanently half *slave* and half *free*."[47]

A week after the nomination, Douglass described Lincoln as "one of the most frank, honest men in political life." The editor said he wished the Republican Party would inscribe on its banner "Death to Slavery" instead of "No more Slave States." However, he wrote that "in the absence of all hope of rearing up the standard of such a party for the coming campaign, we can but desire the success of the Republican candidates." Edmund Quincy, editor of the *Anti-Slavery Standard*, was less sanguine. He said the country would be treated to political speeches and campaign pamphlets about slavery, but, when November came, the result would be "the election of a new administration pledged to the support of slavery in our Southern States . . . whether success be to the Democrats or the Republicans."[48]

Although Garrison still had harsh words for Republicans, he hoped a victory would check the spread of slavery by a show of political strength to the belligerent South. He argued that Republicans could "create such a moral and religious sentiment against slavery as shall mould all parties and sects to effect its overthrow." As the election drew closer, Garrison was gratified to see public opinion changing. The pending election, he wrote in September, revealed "a marked division between the political forces of the North and of the South; and though it relates, ostensibly, solely to the question of the further extension of slavery, it really signifies a much deeper sentiment in the breasts of the people of the North, which, in process of time, must ripen into more decisive action." The *Independent's* Theodore Tilton heartily agreed. He said the election had come to be all about the future of slavery, and Republicans must meet the issue head-on. "All forms of opposition to the Republicans rest upon the fact that the question of slavery is the only real issue in the Presidential election," he wrote. "The Republicans can defeat the combined opposition by resolutely and earnestly meeting that issue. If they make this subordinate to other questions, or if they fail to deal with this as if they were really in earnest to rid the Federal Government of all complicity with slavery, then either Mr. Lincoln will be defeated by the people, or his election will be equivalent to defeat, dishonor, and disruption."[49]

The historic 1860 election became a four-man race when members of the old Whig Party reorganized as the Constitutional Union Party and nominated John Bell of Tennessee as their nominee. This aging group of conservatives, sometimes known as the Old Gentlemen's Party, took no stand on the issue of slavery. They adopted a platform pledging "to recognize no principle other than *the Constitution . . . the Union . . . and the Enforcement of the Laws.*" Recognizing that they could not win the election, their goal was to deny all four candidates a majority of electoral votes so that the race would be thrown into the House of Representatives. There they hoped the crisis over slavery could reach a compromise.

The election reflected just how sectionalized the country had become. The race in the North pitted Douglas against Lincoln, and in the South Breckenridge against Bell. Southern rights leaders again voiced their threats to secede from the Union if the Republicans were victorious. However, Northerners had heard such warnings for years and argued they were merely a bluff. Lincoln's stunning victory—he captured every state but one in the North while not winning a single state in the South— produced mixed feelings among abolitionist editors. The first Republican president certainly was no radical abolitionist who was going to end slavery immediately—and most editors recognized that. But after swimming against the country's political tide for so long, editors said abolitionists could congratulate themselves.

"Our readers know that we expect little or no Anti-Slavery help from Mr. Lincoln, but we none the less recognize his election as an Anti-Slavery triumph and the result of long Anti-Slavery labors," wrote Quincy in the *Anti-Slavery Standard*. "It is not the harvest, but it is the green blade that must go before it." Douglass rejoiced that the Republican victory meant the slave power no longer ruled the country. "Lincoln's election has vitiated their authority and broken their power," he wrote in his monthly. "More important still, it has demonstrated the possibility of electing, if not an Abolitionist, at least an *anti-slavery reputation* to the Presidency." The *Independent* said the historic election meant that the federal government would now be committed to "an honest and capable devotion to the righteous ends of government under a Constitution of Freedom." Slaves were not yet free, the paper declared, "yet the day of their safe and peaceable emancipation will be visibly hastened by the inauguration of an era of freedom at Washington."[50]

The angry reaction of the South to Lincoln's election delighted Garrison and other abolitionist editors. Led by long-belligerent South Carolina, several Southern states immediately began talking about leaving the Union. "The brutal dastards and blood-minded tyrants, who have so long ruled the country with impunity, are now furiously foaming at the mouth, gnawing their tongues for pain, indulging in the most horrid blasphemies, uttering the wildest threats and avowing the most treasonable designs," Garrison wrote in the *Liberator*. "They rave just as fiercely as though he [Lincoln] were another John Brown, armed for Southern invasion and universal emancipation!" When the Palmetto State seceded before the end of the year, Garrison rejoiced heartily. "At last, 'the covenant with death' is annulled . . . at last, by the action of South Carolina, and, ere long, by all the slaveholding States for their doom is one," he proclaimed. "Hail the approaching jubilee, ye millions who are wearing the galling chains of slavery; for, assuredly, the day of your redemption draws nigh, bringing liberty to you, and salvation to the whole land!" The next four years would indeed spell doom for slavery in the United States. But not even the prescient Garrison knew how much blood would be spilled before that happened.[51]

SEVEN

WAR AND EMANCIPATION

Three months after Abraham Lincoln's election led South Carolina batteries in Charleston harbor to fire on Fort Sumter, the *Liberator* printed a long editorial with the headline, "The Flag of Our Union—What Does It Symbolize?" The editorial questioned whether federal troops would be fighting a war with the South for freedom or slavery. It posed other queries: Would the states in rebellion be brought back into a Union that permitted them the right to enslave blacks? Or had the rebellion presented the country with the opportunity for a new birth of freedom?[1]

As the country prepared for a war it had desperately sought to avoid, few Americans wanted to address these difficult questions. Certainly not congressional leaders who tried to pass various compromise packages aimed at appeasing the rebellious South; certainly not the conservatives of the North, who blamed abolitionists for the secession crisis and encouraged a new wave of mob violence; and certainly not a cautious President Lincoln who, despite his hatred of slavery, wanted above everything else to save the Union.

But through their various newspapers, abolitionist editors not only raised the questions, but kept on raising them during four years of a costly civil war. They fought to free the slaves and for a constitutional amendment that would officially end the institution. They fought for the right of blacks to enlist in the military and for black soldiers to receive the same pay as whites. And they fought for full equality of blacks at the ballot box, on public transportation, and in other areas of life. Significantly, the abolitionist press was regularly joined by outspoken and influential Republican newspapers. But as they had done for four decades, antislavery publications, more often than not, spoke first and loudest.

Abolitionist editors opposed all attempts at compromise during the secession winter of 1860–61. The Crittenden Compromise, sponsored by Senator John Crittenden of Kentucky, was the most comprehensive of these measures. It proposed a set of six amendments to the Constitution that would have protected slavery in states against future interference, prohibited slavery in states north of 36°30′, and protected it south of the line in all territories "now held or hereafter acquired." With few exceptions, abolitionist editors assailed the measure. "In vain have been, and will be, all compromises between North and South," William Lloyd Garrison wrote. "All Union-saving efforts are simply idiotic." The editor declared, "At last 'the covenant with death' is annulled, and 'the agreement with hell' broken. The people of the North should recognize the fact that THE UNION IS DISSOLVED, and act accordingly." Frederick Douglass wrote that "if the Union can only be maintained by new concessions to the slaveholders; if it can only be stuck together and held together by a new drain on the negro's blood . . . then will every right minded man and woman in the land say, let the Union perish, and perish forever."[2]

But those who supported compromise with the South fought back—literally. During the secession winter, abolitionists faced a wave of violence not seen since the 1830s. Once again led by "gentlemen of property and standing," the mobs were largely made up of people who believed their livelihoods to be threatened by disunion. Often the attacks were fueled by the Democratic press of the North, which blamed abolitionists for the country's deepening crisis. The *Providence Daily Post* asked if the Northern people would consent to a dissolution of the Union "merely to please the crazy fanatics who have managed this anti-slavery agitation? Will they make the Negro their god, and give up their natural greatness . . . everything for which, as a people, they have been proud?"[3]

Some of the worst riots took place in Boston. Antislavery supporters in the city held a meeting on December 3, 1860, the anniversary of John Brown's execution. When a mob tried to take over the meeting, abolitionists fought back. Police, who sympathized with the protesters and refused to protect the meeting's organizers, finally stepped in and ordered everybody to go home. Abolitionists continued their meeting at a nearby black church, and afterward the mob attacked blacks as they left the church. The next month, hecklers tried to disrupt the Massachusetts Anti-Slavery Society's meeting in Boston, and police were forced to clear the galleries.[4]

The abolitionist press widely reported the incidents, claiming they were further evidence of what slavery was doing to the country. But unlike three decades earlier, when the mainstream press ignored the riots or supported the mob action, this time Garrison and company were joined by dozens of Republican papers which also decried the violence and spread the news throughout the North. Bolstered by this editorial support, the *Anti-Slavery Standard* congratulated abolitionists for having never had "more abundant reason for satisfaction as to the past and hope as to the future than they have now."[5]

Even as one Southern state after another left the Union during the winter, abolitionist editors did not expect that the nation would go to war. After years of giving in to Southern demands on issue after issue, most believed that the North lacked the will and courage to fight. Moreover, they claimed that the myriad compromises being offered showed just how far the country's leaders were willing to give in to Southern demands. "All talk about putting down treason and rebellion by force is as impotent and worthless as the words of a drunken woman in a ditch," a dismissive Douglass wrote.[6]

But then on April 12 Confederate cannons opened fire on Fort Sumter, and the next day the fort's beleaguered federal garrison was forced to surrender. Patriotism swept the North as tens of thousands of volunteers responded to President Lincoln's call to put down the insurrection. Astounded abolitionist editors were overjoyed. "What a change now greets us," Douglass proclaimed in his monthly. "The Government is aroused, the dead North is alive, and its divided people united . . . The cry now is for war, vigorous war, war to the bitter end, and war till the traitors are effectually and permanently put down." Garrison, the man who had always preached the peaceful overthrow of slavery, promptly did an about-face. He described the war sentiment as "total, wonderful, indescribable—uniting the most discordant, and reconciling the most estranged."[7]

The abolitionist press recognized that the war would be fought to restore the Union and that few people in the North believed that emancipation should be a goal of the fighting. But editors also predicted that slavery would be crippled, if not eliminated entirely, as a result of the war. "This outburst of spirit and enthusiasm in the North may spring chiefly from indignation at the wrongs of the white man," declared the *Anti-Slavery Standard,* "but it will none the less finally right those of the black man." Abolitionists embraced the war as a way to end slavery once and for all. In an editorial entitled "The Second American Revolution," William Goodell wrote, "It has begun . . . The Revolution must go on, to its completion—a National *Abolition of Slavery* . . . What but the insanity of moral blindness can long delay the proclamation, inviting [the slaves] to a share in the *glorious second American Revolution.*" The *Anglo-African,* a weekly for blacks in New York founded in 1859, argued that the black man's "title to life, to liberty and the pursuit of happiness must be acknowledged, or the nation will be forsworn; and being so, incur the dreadful penalty of permanent disunion, unending anarchy, and perpetual strife."[8]

Abolitionist editors celebrated the war enthusiasm that seemed to be galvanizing the North. On the first page of his monthly, Douglass inserted drawings of an American eagle and the flag, accompanied by the caption, "Freedom for all, or chains for all." When the popular abolitionist lecturer Wendell Phillips gave a ringing endorsement of the war to an enthusiastic audience, the *Liberator* published an extra edition containing his speech, and newsboys sold 16,000 copies of the paper. The *Anti-Slavery Standard, Anglo-African,* and several daily newspapers also reprinted the speech.

During the early months of the war, the abolitionist press urged supporters to put aside any criticism of the president or his administration in order to show unanimity against the South.

The American and New England Anti-Slavery societies even took the unprecedented step of canceling their annual meetings in order to avoid any possible controversy. The *Anti-Slavery Standard* conceded that agitation had always been one of the chief duties of the organization. "But, in a crisis like this, criticism may suspend its judgment for awhile and watch the sequence of events," the newspaper announced.[9]

However, antislavery editors did not check their criticism for long. When Garrisonians held their annual Fourth of July picnic in 1861, many spoke out against their leader's support for the war effort. They argued that until the government proclaimed emancipation to be a goal of the fighting, abolitionists should not support it. The *Liberator* reported on the criticism, as well as the response of Garrison and others. For his part, Garrison declared that if the government tried to end the war with slavery secure, "then will be the time for me to open all the guns that I can bring to bear on it." But, he wrote, "blessed be God, that the 'covenant with death' has been annulled, and that 'agreement with hell' no longer stands. I joyfully accept the fact, and leave all verbal criticism until a more suitable opportunity."[10]

Hopes for a quick war ended with the North's embarrassing defeat at the First Battle of Bull Run. However, shrewd abolitionists recognized that this loss would force the Northern people, in the words of James M. McPherson, "to reassess their war policy and to reflect more seriously on the slavery issue." Both the abolitionist and mainstream press reported that more people in the North were expressing abolitionist views. Douglass believed that the defeat had "changed the tone of Northern sentiment as to the proper mode of prosecuting the war . . . A cry has gone forth for the abolition of slavery." The Republican *Philadelphia Inquirer* said the Union could learn a valuable lesson from the rout at Bull Run. "Let us take comfort that we now know the worst," the newspaper said. "It is better that this rebellion should have first victories than the last . . . This very seeming defeat will but be turned into a source of future triumph, if we profit by its lessons. Nations, as well as individuals, sometimes need the discipline of misfortune."[11]

Abolitionists soon renewed their call that emancipation must be an aim of the war. They developed the argument that slavery was both a source of strength and weakness to the Confederacy. Antislavery publications began quoting from Southern newspapers such as the *Montgomery Advertiser,* which proclaimed that slavery was a "tower of strength to the Confederacy." White men were freed to enlist in the army, according to the paper, because slaves took care of the wartime labor. Certainly, Douglass recognized that slavery was a source of manpower for the Confederacy. He hammered home this theme in repeated editorials. "Why? Oh! Why, in the name of all that is national, does our Government allow its enemies this powerful advantage?" Douglass wrote. "The very stomach of this rebellion is the negro in the condition of the slave. Arrest that hoe in the hands of the negro, and you smite the rebellion in the very seat of its life."[12]

In August, Union general John C. Frémont declared martial law in Missouri and issued an order freeing the slaves of all rebels in the state. Abolitionist publications hailed the proclamation. They were joined by many Republican and even a few Democratic newspapers. However, a cautious President Lincoln was concerned that Frémont's order would alarm the crucial border state of Kentucky, which had considerable Southern sympathies. He asked the general to make the order consistent with the federal confiscation policy. When Frémont refused, the president modified it to confiscate only those slaves who had aided Confederate forces. He also reassigned the popular Frémont to a post in western Virginia.

The antislavery press was furious. The *Anti-Slavery Standard* called Lincoln's move "one of those blunders which are worse than crimes." Garrison published the president's order and put thick black rules around it, the traditional newspaper sign of mourning. He said the president was guilty of "a serious dereliction of duty. Either the government must abolish slavery, or the independence of the Southern Confederacy must be recognized." And Douglass asked, "What is the friendship of these so-called loyal slaveholders worth? The open hostility of these so-called loyal slaveholders is incomparably to be preferred to their friendship. They are far more easily dealt with and disposed of as enemies than as allies. From the beginning, these border Slave States have been the mill-stone about the neck of the Government."[13]

Frustrated with the immediate prospects for emancipation, abolitionists inaugurated new efforts to force Lincoln into taking action. Massachusetts abolitionists formed the Emancipation League, which sponsored a lecture series, started a new petition drive, and created a new weekly antislavery newspaper, the *Boston Commonwealth*. Goodell organized a National Emancipation Association in New York. And a group of antislavery leaders in Washington started the Washington Lecture Association. The abolitionist press widely publicized these activities.

Another important abolitionist voice also emerged during this time, the *Independent*. The weekly had been founded in 1848 as a Congregational antislavery journal and had grown to become the largest religious publication in the country. During its first decade, the newspaper's primary concern was the growth of the Congregationalist church. Under the editorship of three clergymen, the *Independent* pursued a generally conservative course with respect to abolition, and as late as 1860 it refused to support full emancipation. Then in early 1861, the three clergymen resigned and Henry Ward Beecher was named editor. Beecher's editorials had already made him popular with the newspaper's readers. But with his busy schedule, Beecher soon turned over many of his editorial duties to Theodore Tilton, a young abolitionist who had worked for the paper since 1856.

More than six feet tall, with flowing hair and a magnetic personality, Tilton quickly made his presence felt. Tilton was a talented writer, and under his direction the *Independent* became increasingly radical in its calls for emancipation. Amidst the lengthy sermons, Christian-inspired poetry, and other religious materials, Tilton printed damning condemnations of slavery and slaveholders. When the press carried stories about slave catchers coming into the nation's capital and seizing slaves on the streets, the paper asked, "Is it possible that such a deed can be perpetrated by the Government and not be branded by the nation as a disgrace?" Tilton eventually became the paper's editor, and for the rest of the war abolitionists could count on him to wholeheartedly support their work.[14]

In late 1861 Garrison changed the longtime slogan on the *Liberator*'s banner. He removed the "covenant with death" message and replaced it with the biblical command from the book of Leviticus: "Proclaim Liberty throughout all the land, to all the inhabitants thereof." When critics complained that he appeared to be now supporting a government that still permitted slavery, Garrison responded in uncharacteristically

humorous fashion. He said that when he vowed in 1844 not to
sustain the Constitution because it was "a covenant with death
and an agreement with hell," he had "no idea that [he] would
live to see death and hell secede."[15]

Garrison used the amusing remark in the growing number of
venues across the North where he was invited to speak. Starting
in the fall of 1861, Garrison and other abolitionists enjoyed a
popularity they had never experienced before. Antislavery
speakers were greeted enthusiastically in places where mobs had
once ruled. Goodell was moved to write: "Never has there been
a time when Abolitionists were as much respected, as at present.
Never has there been a time in which their strongest and most
radical utterances . . . were as readily received by the people, as
at present . . . Announce the presence of a competent abolition
lecturer and the house is crammed."[16]

But the growing esteem for abolitionists did not immediately
translate into success in getting the administration to change
its views on emancipation. In his annual message to Congress
on December 3, 1861, the president declared that "the Union
must be preserved, and hence, all indispensable means must be
employed. We should not be in haste to determine that radical
and extreme measures, which may reach the loyal as well as the
disloyal, are indispensable." Lincoln's only reference to emancipation was a recommendation that the United States acquire
territory to colonize slaves freed by the Confiscation Act, which
allowed slaves and other property used in the Confederate war
effort to be seized. Abolitionist editors were outraged. Douglass
said that "the friends of freedom, the Union and the Constitution,
have been most basely betrayed, deceived and swindled." The
administration, he wrote, had shown itself to be "destitute of
any anti-slavery principle or feeling." And Garrison groused, "If

there be not soon an 'irrepressible conflict' in the Republican ranks, in regard to his course of policy, I shall almost despair of the country."[17]

Congress, however, was taking steps toward emancipation, even if the president seemingly was not. In the spring lawmakers passed several antislavery bills, including a measure to prohibit slavery in all U.S. territories and another to free all slaves in the District of Columbia. Abolitionist editors, who for decades had been calling for an end to slavery in the nation's capital, praised the measures and kept up pressure on the president.

However, other events deeply disturbed abolitionists. In April, Major General David Hunter, commander of the Union forces occupying the islands and coastline of Florida, Georgia, and South Carolina, proclaimed martial law in those areas. Then on May 9, without the approval of Congress or the president, Hunter declared all slaves in the three states to be "forever free" and authorized arming all able-bodied black men in those states. Bowing to pressure from Unionists in the border states, the president revoked Hunter's order. Also that spring came the news that slave catchers were seizing blacks on the streets of the nation's capital, claiming they were fugitives. With the Union army unable to win a significant victory in Virginia and Confederate general Robert E. Lee grabbing attention for his bold leadership on the battlefield, the abolitionist press demanded the president take decisive action on the issue of emancipation.[18]

Lincoln finally decided to act. In July, the president submitted the first draft of an emancipation proclamation to his cabinet. Members discussed the timing of any announcement, and Secretary of State Seward persuaded Lincoln to withhold it until Union forces won a major victory on the battlefield.

None of this behind-the-scenes maneuvering was known to abolitionist editors, who continued their blistering criticism of the president. Garrison called Lincoln's course on emancipation "stumbling, halting, prevaricating, irresolute, weak, [and] besotted." Many newspapers published excerpts from a thundering speech by Phillips in which he called Lincoln a "first-rate *second-rate* man."[19]

The *New York Tribune*'s Horace Greeley was also becoming increasingly impatient with the president. In August he wrote his famous editorial, "The Prayer of Twenty Millions," demanding ungrudging execution of the confiscation laws granting freedom to the slaves of those resisting the Union. The savvy president, who had once said that having the popular Greeley behind him would "be as helpful as an army of one hundred thousand men," knew he must publicly respond to the editor. Lincoln answered back in the *National Intelligencer* with one of his most memorable public statements. "My paramount object in this struggle *is* to save the Union, and is *not* either to save or to destroy slavery," Lincoln wrote. "If I could save the Union without freeing *any* slave I would do it, and if I could save it by freeing *all* the slaves, I would do it; and if I could save it by freeing some and leaving others alone, I would also do that."[20]

Reaction to the president's reply varied among abolitionist editors. A bitter Edmund Quincy wrote sarcastically in the *Anti-Slavery Standard* that since thus far in the war Lincoln had failed to save the Union without freeing any slaves, perhaps the president should now see if emancipating some would have better results. But others saw some hope in the president's response.[21]

Then on September 17, the Union beat back the Confederacy's invasion of the North at the battle of Antietam, and the president unexpectedly issued his preliminary Emancipation Proclamation five days later. The proclamation announced that on January 1, 1863, all slaves in the rebel states "shall be then, thenceforward and forever, free." Loyal slave states and any rebellious states which returned to the Union before that time would be exempt, but Lincoln also promised to present a plan for the gradual, compensated emancipation of slaves in the loyal states.[22]

Most antislavery editors hailed the announcement. "We shout with joy that we live to record this righteous decree," wrote Douglass. An ecstatic Greeley proclaimed, "It is the beginning of the end of the rebellion; the beginning of the new life of the nation. GOD BLESS ABRAHAM LINCOLN!" Tilton declared the proclamation "the most important paper ever published in the *Independent*—the most extraordinary document ever proceeding from this government." He likened the proclamation to "the drawing of a sword that can never be sheathed again. The very existence of the loyal States will now depend on the enforcement of this decree." The *Chicago Tribune,* one of the administration's most loyal supporters among the Republican press, declared that the president had "set his hand and affixed the great seal of the nation to the grandest proclamation ever issued by man . . . From the date of this proclamation begins the history of the republic as our fathers designed to have it— the home of freedom, the asylum of the oppressed, the seat of justice, the land of equal rights under the law, where each man, however humble, shall be entitled to life, liberty, and the pursuit of happiness." However, Garrison's reaction was more luke-warm. The editor said the proclamation was a "step in the right direction," but he maintained it did not go far enough. In his view, the document only proved that Lincoln would do nothing directly for the slaves, but pursued policies "only by circumlo-cution and delay."[23]

Garrison showed far more excitement after the final Emancipation Proclamation was announced on January 1, 1863. With a fresh snow covering the ground, hundreds of anti-slavery supporters packed Boston's Tremont Temple to await the announcement. Banners hung from the temple's columns, and an orchestra played Mendelssohn's "Hymn of Praise." After speeches by Douglass, Ralph Waldo Emerson, and others, a courier brought the news that the president had signed the proc-lamation. The temple erupted in pandemonium. The crowd yelled, "Three times three for Lincoln" and then "Three cheers for Garrison." From the gallery, the editor simply waved and smiled. The next day, Garrison went to the *Liberator*'s office and with his own hands proudly set the type for the headline that read: "The Proclamation. Three Million of Slaves Set Free! Glory Hallelujah!"[24]

For most abolitionists, simply freeing blacks was not enough. They wanted equality for the race. The *Independent*'s Tilton expressed the views of many. "This is a war not of geographical sections, not of political factions, but of principles and systems," he wrote in 1863. "Our war against this rebellion . . . is a war for social equality, for rights, for justice, for freedom." Some strides for blacks had been achieved in the decades before the war, but they still suffered from many forms of discrimination. Blacks could not vote in some Northern states, and most public schools outside of New England were still segregated. Discriminatory public transportation laws remained on the books in New York, Philadelphia, Cincinnati, and other major cities. Blacks were also denied entrance to many hotels, restaurants, and recre-ational facilities throughout the North.[25]

Antislavery editors publicized the work of abolitionists who were fighting against discrimination and prejudice. Often this was done by individuals or small groups working quietly. In 1865 the chaplain of the House of Representatives invited a black minister to take the pulpit for a Sunday morning service. Editors also exulted when John Rock of Boston became the first black attorney to be accredited to argue cases before the United States Supreme Court.

Editors also publicized the work of abolitionists to desegregate schools in the North. Although some cities had abolished segregation in public schools, many others maintained separate systems for whites and blacks. Abolitionists kept steady pressure on school officials and local legislators to end the practice, arguing that black schools received inferior support. As a result, Connecticut and Rhode Island eventually abolished segregated public education.

Some of the greatest successes came in fighting segregation in public transportation. Several abolitionist publications in New York City campaigned to abolish laws segregating, and, in some cases, banning, blacks from the city's streetcars. Editors argued that the streetcars were common carriers and thus required by law to provide transportation to all citizens. After the papers publicized some ugly incidents, including one in which the widow of a black soldier was kicked off a bus, the streetcar company gave up its discriminatory practices. In Philadelphia, the abolitionist press published stories of wounded black soldiers being ejected from the city's horsecars. A mass meeting was held in January 1865 and adopted resolutions calling on the railroad companies to stop their discriminatory policies. When the companies refused and were supported by the city's mayor, abolitionists took the fight to the state legislature and eventually won a law prohibiting discrimination in public transportation in the entire state of Pennsylvania. In a series of editorials, the *New York Tribune* supported Charles Sumner's attack on the segregation of the horsecars and railroads in the District of Columbia. After two years, a bill passed prohibiting segregation on streetcars in the district. The *Liberator's* headline proclaimed, "A Blow at Complexional Caste."[26]

Abolitionist editors angrily condemned the draft riots that took place in New York City in July 1863. The riots occurred because working-class New Yorkers, especially Irish Catholics, believed that Protestants were forcing the war on them for the freedom of blacks. They also feared that blacks would take their jobs at lower wages. During four days of street violence, hundreds of rioters looted the homes of prominent citizens and burned Protestant churches. They also lynched a half-dozen blacks and burned several black establishments, including the Colored Orphan Asylum. Before federal troops brought the mob under control, the rioters attacked the homes of abolitionists and tried to wreck the offices of the *New York Tribune*. In all, an estimated 1,000 people were killed, including ten policemen and soldiers. Greeley argued that resistance of the draft was "merely the occasion of the outbreak; absolute disloyalty and hatred to the Negro were the moving cause." The *Liberator* echoed that sentiment, saying that the draft was "only the pretext, not the real cause for this treasonable outbreak." It said the real cause was the "brutal hatred of the colored race, and, consequently, of all efforts for the abolition of slavery."[27]

From the beginning of the war, many abolitionists believed that black men should be able to enlist in the military, arguing that this would strike another blow at slavery. Within days of Lincoln's initial call for troops in 1861, blacks in Boston, Philadelphia, and other cities organized militia units. Douglass, for one, passionately believed that black troops could provide a tremendous advantage for the Union in fighting the Confederacy. In an editorial titled "How to End the War," the editor said the North could win by "carrying the war into Africa." "Let the slaves and free colored people be called into service and formed into a liberating army," he wrote, "to march into the South and raise the banner of Emancipation among the slaves."[28]

Lincoln initially opposed enlisting black troops because he feared such a federal policy would arouse prejudices and anger the border states. Abolitionist editors replied angrily. Douglass said keeping blacks out of the military was like fighting "with only One Hand." "What upon earth is the matter with the American government and people," he asked in his monthly. "Why does the Government reject the negro? Is he not a man? Can he not wield a sword, fire a gun, march and countermarch, and obey orders like any others?"[29]

But as weariness with the war set in and the military found it increasingly hard to find volunteers, the administration's attitude began to change. The secretary of war authorized the Union military governor of South Carolina's Sea Islands to raise black regiments. Commanded by abolitionist Thomas Wentworth Higginson, the blacks proved to be excellent soldiers. Higginson praised the courage of the troops in his reports, which were printed by the abolitionist press.[30]

More than any other antislavery editor, Douglass beat the drum for enlisting black troops. In March 1863 he published one of his best-known editorials, "Men of Color to Arms!" The editor urged his fellow blacks to "fly to arms, and smite with death the power that would bury the government and your liberty in the same hopeless grave." Douglass said it was far better for black men to die free than to live as slaves. "Liberty won only by white men will lose half its luster," he wrote. "Who would be free themselves must strike the blow."[31]

Douglass then set out to enlist black recruits, and by mid-April he had sent more than 100 men to serve in the 54th Massachusetts Regiment. The abolitionist press celebrated when the 54th Massachusetts became the first black regiment to serve in the war. Led by Colonel Robert Gould Shaw, a college graduate and member of one of the state's oldest families, the regiment paraded through downtown Boston before leaving on a transport ship to South Carolina. Among the soldiers were two of Douglass's sons. The scene of black men in uniform marching to the music of "John Brown's Body" as thousands of residents looked on was an impressive sight, and abolitionist editors gushed with pride.

The 54th Massachusetts performed heroically that summer in a nighttime assault on Fort Wagner, a beachfront artillery post guarding Charleston's harbor. In a frontal attack with hand-to-hand fighting, the regiments gained the fort's parapet and held it for an hour before falling back. But the assault came at a frightful cost as the 54th lost nearly half its men, including Colonel Shaw, who was killed leading the charge. (Neither of Douglass's sons was injured.) Editors virtually canonized Shaw and his black troops for their valor. The *Anti-Slavery Standard* declared that Fort Wagner was a "holy sepulchre" to the black race. The battle made Fort Wagner "such a name to the colored race as Bunker Hill has been for ninety years to the white Yankees," said the *New York Tribune*.[32]

Although the enlistment of black troops in the Union army was gratifying to abolitionist editors, the pay and treatment of the soldiers was not. Black soldiers were often assigned posts in some of the most difficult locations. Their equipment and weapons were old and outdated. Even more appalling to blacks was the pay. Black troops were paid $10 per month, $3 of which could be deducted for clothing. On the other hand, whites received $13 per month, plus a clothing allowance of $3. The pay scale had been set up early in the war, when blacks were expected to serve in the army as laborers and not as soldiers. However, there was no attempt to rectify the inequality, and abolitionist editors were outraged. In December 1863, Secretary of War Edwin Stanton asked Congress to approve a bill to grant equal pay to black troops. A bill was introduced, but it stalled in the face of opposition from members who claimed that paying blacks the same wages as whites would demean white troops.[33]

Abolitionist newspapers criticized the conservative congressmen who were blocking the measure. "It is time this fooling with the black man was done with," the *Chicago Tribune* editorialized. "If he earns wages, why not pay them to him? If he earns as much as a man of any other color, why not pay him as much?" The *Anglo-African* published a letter from a black soldier stationed in Florida describing the hardships that the families of black soldiers faced. Nonetheless, he reported, many of the black soldiers were refusing to accept any pay until they received the same amount as whites. "Our debasement is most complete," he wrote. "No chance for promotion, no money for our families, and we little better than an armed band of laborers with rusty muskets and bright spades, what is our incentive to duty. Yet

God has put it into our hearts to believe that we will survive or perish with the liberty of our country."[34]

In the summer of 1864, Congress passed legislation equalizing the pay of black and white troops. The law provided that blacks free on April 19, 1861, were entitled to full pay retroactive to January 1, 1864. Abolitionist editors fought against the retroactive date because some black regiments in the South were mustered in before 1864. In the last month of the war, a law granting full retroactive pay for all black soldiers passed.

For Douglass, the enlistment of black troops was the last major crusade in his career as an editor. His publication had become a monthly in 1859 after years of increasing debt. Even then the debts grew, and by 1863 Douglass had tired of the financial struggle. In August he announced that he was publishing the last issue of *Douglass' Monthly,* saying there were now several publications in which blacks could express their views. Douglass devoted the rest of his life to the causes of free blacks, most notably the right to vote.[35]

As the year 1864 began, President Lincoln faced the real danger that he would not be reelected or even renominated. The Republican Party was largely a collection of political factions, and by 1862 a powerful group of radicals had emerged. The radicals had long been critical of Lincoln's conduct of the war. The group, which included some in the abolitionist press, also believed the president had not moved fast enough in ending slavery and was too conservative on the issue of equal rights for blacks. By 1864 they wanted a new nominee, and they had precedent on their side. No president since Andrew Jackson had won a second term.

Lincoln's opponents were particularly disappointed in the reconstruction policy he announced in 1863, believing it did not go far enough in securing equal rights for newly freed blacks. Several Republicans were interested in securing the nomination, including General Frémont and Treasury Secretary Salmon P. Chase. Chase, one of the most ambitious politicians of his era, was perhaps the abolitionist movement's strongest ally in the cabinet. The *Independent* was sympathetic to the Chase movement, and in early 1864 the paper called for the nomination of a man committed to equal rights in solution to the reconstruction problem. While not mentioning the president by name, the paper said Lincoln did not fulfill the requirement while Chase did. But the secretary's candidacy ended amid charges of corruption in the Treasury Department. Frémont, the 1856 Republican nominee and now a disgruntled Union general because he had been relieved of his command in Missouri, had support from some publications.

Garrison steadfastly supported Lincoln's renomination, even though many members of the Massachusetts Anti-Slavery Society, most notably the radical Phillips, did not back the president. Garrison refused to support a resolution by the society in January 1864 condemning the administration for its weak reconstruction policy, and the *Liberator* reprinted the rancorous debate between Garrison and Phillips over the issue. Phillips claimed the administration was "ready to sacrifice the interest and honor of the North to secure a sham peace" that would betray equal rights for blacks. He claimed that the president had no desire to elevate free blacks to a "higher status, social or political, than that of a mere labourer, superintended by others." Garrison conceded that Lincoln's reconstruction policy was not ideal. But the editor argued that the president was committed to emancipation and that his reelection was the wisest course for the country.[36]

Abolitionist editors downplayed the rift between the movement's two giants. Antislavery supporters always debated issues passionately, they said, and this was just the latest example of that. The "cheerful caution of Mr. Garrison" and the "less hopeful doubtings of Mr. Phillips" work together for the good of the cause, said the *Anti-Slavery Standard*. For his part, Garrison said Phillips was free to express any opinion he wished.[37]

But Garrison also warned against Republican factionalism that might cause the party to lose the White House that year. Although Lincoln was not perfect, Garrison wrote in an editorial, there was still "much to rejoice over and be thankful for." The president's many errors could be excused for one who "at one blow, severed the chains of three millions three hundred thousand slaves," he argued. The editor, who for many years had felt nothing but disdain for political candidates or parties, was becoming a full-fledged Republican.[38]

As some of the bloodiest fighting of the war took place at Spotsylvania Court House, and as the Union Army began its Atlanta campaign, the debate over Lincoln's renomination continued at the annual meetings of both the American Anti-Slavery Society and the New England Anti-Slavery Society in May. The anti-Lincoln side continued to be led by Phillips, while Garrison headed the president's supporters. The abolitionist press covered the passionate speeches of both factions at the meetings. In the end, both societies approved resolutions criticizing the president but only by small margins.[39]

Antislavery newspapers reported on the convention in Cleveland where Frémont was nominated as the candidate of the new Radical Democratic Party. Abolitionists were disappointed that the party's platform did not endorse black suffrage, but they were pleased that it called for a constitutional amendment to prohibit slavery and secure equal rights for all men. Supporters believed that the Cleveland meeting would force the Republicans to adopt a more radical platform on the issues of slavery and Reconstruction than they otherwise would have done.

Despite the competition from Frémont, Lincoln was unanimously renominated by Republicans at their convention in Baltimore. Garrison attended the party's convention with Tilton, and the *Liberator*'s editor was warmly greeted by the delegates, who called his name from the floor. Garrison was overcome with emotion as he watched the delegates adopt a resolution pledging the party to end slavery by a constitutional amendment. The "whole body of delegates sprang to their feet" when the resolution was read, Garrison wrote in the *Liberator*. "Was not a spectacle like that rich compensation for more than thirty years of universal personal opprobrium?"[40]

For the next three months, the antislavery press poured out editorials arguing over which candidate would be better for blacks. Tilton and Phillips debated the candidates and platforms in the pages of the *Independent,* and the exchange was widely reprinted by the Northern press. Phillips decried Republicans for their conservatism and praised the Cleveland platform for its commitment to guarantee equality before the law. "There can be no possible salvation for the Union, and no safety for the negro in his freedom, except on the basis of every man of every race equal in privilege, right and franchise before the law," he wrote. Tilton accused Frémont's supporters of being allied with Copperhead Democrats whose only interest was in defeating the Republicans. "Now we would be glad if a great political party could go before the country on the high issue of giving every black man a vote," he wrote. "But the country is not ready for such an issue . . . If the next election were to turn upon the question of giving every black man a vote, the Copperheads would achieve the next administration."[41]

In the meantime, the news from the battlefield was not good for Republican hopes of holding onto the White House. The mounting casualty figures, and Union stalemates in Virginia and outside Atlanta, had caused Northern morale to plummet. Democrats had nominated the popular General George B. McClellan as their candidate, and they sensed victory. A despondent Lincoln wrote a memorandum stating that he would probably not be reelected. Abolitionist editors debated about whether the Republicans should meet again to nominate a new candidate who might allow the party to hold on to the White House. Then came the news on September 3 that after a long siege, the Union army had captured the important Southern city of Atlanta. Across the North despair suddenly turned into unbridled joy.

The antislavery press reveled in the news from Atlanta, sensing what it meant for Lincoln's chances in November. The *Philadelphia Inquirer* argued that Republican leaders had long been out of step regarding popular opinion of the president. "Whatever may be the differences of opinion as to his policy or his administrative ability," the paper declared, "it is clear that he has a powerful hold on the popular heart; in his integrity and patriotism, and the absolute singleness of purpose with which he has striven for three long years to restore the Union." The influential *New York Tribune* came out in support of the president, arguing that despite Lincoln's faults he was far better than a Copperhead Democrat. In an editorial attributed to Greeley, but actually written by Sydney Gay, the paper declared, "Henceforth we fly the banner of ABRAHAM LINCOLN." The *Tribune* said that Lincoln had "done seven-eighths of the work after his fashion; there must be vigor and virtue enough left in him to do the other fraction . . . We MUST re-elect him, and, God helping us, we WILL." For his part, Greeley thereafter worked tirelessly for the president. The editor spoke repeatedly at Republican gatherings, printed campaign literature, and raised money for the Lincoln campaign.[42]

The *Liberator,* which thanks to Garrison had become every bit a Lincoln organ, insisted that antislavery supporters must keep the president in the White House. Garrison warned readers against "magnifying to huge dimensions those incidental errors and outrages which are inevitable in the midst of such awful civil war," and encouraged them instead to "fix your gaze upon those sublime and glorious acts of President Lincoln's administration, where slavery has received its death warrant, and the haughty Slave Power has been laid low in the dust." At the same time, antislavery editors increasingly urged Frémont to withdraw from the race for the good of the country. On September 17, the general reluctantly pulled out and grudgingly urged his supporters to back the president.[43]

The abolitionist press proclaimed Lincoln's overwhelming victory in November—the president won all but three states—as a triumph for the antislavery cause. By the time he was sworn in, Lincoln was being hailed by many editors as one of the greatest leaders in the country's history. His second inaugural address, with the ringing words, "With malice toward none, with charity for all; with firmness in the right, as God gives us to see the right, let us strive on to finish the work we are in; to bind up the nation's wounds," deserved to be "printed in gold," one antislavery publication declared.[44]

Fulfilling his promise to abolitionist supporters, Lincoln immediately devoted his attention to passage of a constitutional amendment that would prohibit slavery in the United States. Many abolitionist leaders, fearful that the Emancipation Proclamation might become difficult to enforce once the war was over, had been pushing for the amendment. Antislavery societies prepared petitions for Congress, and the abolitionist press publicized the petition drive.

The Senate had adopted the Thirteenth Amendment in April 1864, but the measure failed to win the necessary two-thirds majority in the House of Representatives. Republicans controlled the House with just a small majority and most Democrats voted against the amendment. But Lincoln's overwhelming victory convinced many that the public now supported emancipation. After the presidential election, Lincoln and Seward targeted a list of retiring Democrats and lobbied them tirelessly. The efforts paid off when, on January 31, 1865, sixteen Democrats joined all 103 Republicans to pass the amendment by a vote of 119 to 56, sending it on to the states for ratification. When the vote was announced, the gallery erupted and cannons in the city fired a hundred-gun salute. By acclamation, the House adjourned for the rest of the day "in honor of this immortal and sublime event." The *Liberator* proclaimed the amendment's passage "the greatest and most important event in the history of congressional legislation." "Henceforth," the paper said, "in deed and in truth, America is to be 'the land of the FREE.'" And the *New York Times* declared, "With the passage of this amendment, the Republic enters upon a new stage of its great career. It is hereafter to be, what it has never been hitherto, thoroughly democratic—resting on human rights as its basis, and aiming at the greatest good and the highest happiness of all its people."[45]

Abolitionist editors also took an active role in the reconstruction debate that began when it became increasingly apparent that the North would win the war. The antislavery press wanted a reconstruction policy that would best serve the needs of emancipated slaves. Garrison supported radicals in Congress in arguing that the rebel states should not be legally recognized. Congress should decide upon military control for the South and determine the conditions for states to reenter the Union. "No other course can give repose or security for the horrible excesses of those revolted portions of the country," he wrote in the *Liberator*.[46]

In his annual message in December 1864, President Lincoln announced his policy of restoration, which would offer a full pardon to all rebels who would take an oath of future loyalty to the Constitution. Reconstructed states would have to recognize the permanent freedom of former slaves and provide for their education, but otherwise the states could handle the race issue in their own way. Abolitionist editors were divided over the president's generous policy. The *Independent* gave it cautious approval. But the *Anti-Slavery Standard* said that "the proposition to commit the care and education of the freedmen to those revived States is too much like giving the lambs to the nurture and admonition of wolves."[47]

Abolitionist editors also took great satisfaction in the Confederacy's rancorous debate late in the war on whether to arm slaves. The controversial idea had been discussed privately for years, but after the Union began enlisting black troops, some Southern leaders began discussing it publicly. Supporters argued that military necessity required the Confederacy to tap its last source of military manpower. It was far better for the South to lose its slaves, they reasoned, than to lose its freedom. However, opponents claimed that acknowledging that blacks could be soldiers disproved the Southern notion that they could not be anything other than slaves. Enlisting blacks would end the institution of slavery, they countered, and thereby the cherished Southern way of life. "The leaders of the Rebellion are now beginning to experience for the first time the dire troubles of wide and violent political divisions within their little household," declared the *Philadelphia Inquirer* with obvious glee. "Heretofore they have had a fair approach to unanimity, that is, all have been of one mind who dare express an opinion at all. Now that they propose to lay hands on the heretofore inviolable 'nigger,' there is a wide spread revolt. They are now to experience the bitter fruits, within their own lines, of that agitation for 'abolition' on the one side and fire-eating resistance on the other, with which, for a quarter of a century, they made the politics of the United States one unceasing round of horrible discord."[48]

Confederate general Robert E. Lee had been largely silent on the issue, although there had been rumors that he supported arming slaves. Then in early 1865, the beloved general wrote a letter to a Confederate congressional supporter of a black enlistment bill saying the plan was a military necessity. Moreover, Lee said, blacks who enlisted should be free. "It would neither be just nor wise . . . to require them to serve as slaves," the general wrote. The *New York Tribune* noted the irony of the Confederacy now talking about rewarding blacks for their service with the

promise of freedom. "That Slavery is the best possible condition for the Negro, is the first article in the Rebel creed," the
paper editorialized. "That the Negro loves his master above all
men, takes pride in his service, and would by no means accept
freedom if it were offered to him, used to be the second. The
stress of circumstances has somewhat modified this canon; no
one talks for arming Negroes who does not admit or insist that,
to arm them to any purpose, they must be promised freedom."
Even with Lee's support, the Confederate Congress delayed
taking any action to recruit black soldiers. Not until March did
the Congress pass a law arming the slaves, but the measure did
not provide for their emancipation. In the meantime, at Lee's
encouragement, the Virginia legislature passed its own law
enlisting black soldiers without any promise of freedom.[49]

One final attempt at negotiating an end to the war took
place at what became known as the Hampton Roads Peace
Conference. Francis Preston Blair, the patriarch of a powerful
family and an advisor to U.S. presidents since Jackson, believed
that the North and South could be reunited by a joint campaign
to oust the French-supported regime in Mexico. Blair convinced
Lincoln to let him present the proposal to Confederate president
Jefferson Davis. Neither Lincoln nor Davis believed the bizarre
scheme would work, but each thought he could use a peace
conference to his political advantage. Three-member commis-
sions from both sides met on a riverboat near Hampton Roads,
Virginia, on February 3. At the last minute Lincoln decided to
attend the meeting.

One of the major questions in the peace negotiations was the
issue of slavery. Lincoln suggested the possibility of compen-
sating Southern owners for the loss of their slaves. He also said the
Emancipation Proclamation was a wartime measure that would

be terminated after peace had been achieved. But the president insisted that no slaves freed would be re-enslaved. Moreover, the House of Representatives had just approved the Thirteenth Amendment, and its ratification would make all questions about slavery in the future moot. The exasperated Confederate commissioners said they had been offered little beyond unconditional surrender. The four-hour meeting ended with nothing achieved. Antislavery newspapers praised the president for not backing down on the issue of freeing slaves. And they reveled in the angry reaction of a defiant Confederacy, which vowed to never submit to the disgrace of surrender.[50]

The abolitionist press hailed the final days of the war. The capture of Charleston, where the fighting had begun, was particularly sweet. "Babylon Is Fallen!" the *Liberator* proclaimed. "The rebellion is humbled in the city of its first haughtiness." Garrison and Tilton were among the dignitaries invited to Fort Sumter on April 14 to celebrate the raising of the same American flag that had been lowered when the fort fell to Confederate forces four years earlier. Garrison was a center of attention. In a symbolic gesture, the editor visited John C. Calhoun's tomb and declared, "Down in a deeper grave than this slavery has gone, and for it there is no resurrection." He stopped by the old fire-eating *Charleston Courier,* now a loyalist publication, where the printers invited him to set in type part of a speech by Henry Ward Beecher. They all laughed at what the newspaper's Confederate printers would have thought if they found the hated Garrison setting type beside them at the shop. Garrison also attended a rally at Zion's Church attended by hundreds of black residents. During the event, two young girls presented the editor with a floral wreath. Their father, Samuel Dickerson, said to Garrison,

"I have read of your mighty labors . . . and here is your hand-iwork." Dickerson explained that as slaves his daughters had been taken away from him. "Through your instrumentality, under the folds of that glorious flag . . . you have restored them to me." Moved to tears, Garrison later described it as the most "unspeakably satisfying" moment of his career.[51]

In the midst of the Charleston celebration came the shocking news that President Lincoln had been assassinated by John Wilkes Booth, a Southern sympathizer, just days after the Confederacy's surrender at Appomattox Court House on April 9. Like newspapers across the country, abolitionist editors dressed the columns of their publications in thick black rules in honor of the slain president. They extolled the man they once had bitterly criticized, particularly for the Emancipation Proclamation and the Thirteenth Amendment, calling them the crowning acts of his administration. While many in the North called for vengeance against a traitorous South, abolitionist editors feared this would distract attention from the some of the gains being achieved for newly free blacks. Writing in the *Independent,* Tilton argued that the Confederacy should be punished not by prosecuting the rebels but by ending slavery and granting equal rights to the blacks who had once been enslaved.[52]

When the American Anti-Slavery Society met in Boston the following month, the future of the organization was foremost on everyone's mind. Before the annual meeting, Garrison announced that he planned to discontinue the *Liberator* at the end of 1865. After publishing the weekly for 35 years, the editor was exhausted. Moreover, with the Confederacy defeated and slavery abolished, Garrison believed his work and that of the society was completed. The society had been conceived specifically as an antislavery organization, he argued. Although racial equality had not yet been achieved, Garrison admitted, any future work on behalf of free blacks should be left to others.

However, Phillips, Douglass, and other members insisted there was still plenty of work left to do and that the organization must continue fighting to secure full rights for blacks, particularly the right to vote. Slavery might be dead, but widespread prejudice and discrimination persisted in the United States. In such a critical period for the nation, this was no time to retreat from the ideals of the war. To fold up the organization would be to betray the country's blacks. The society must remain vigilant, they argued.

Although Garrison knew that he lacked the votes to dissolve the society, he still moved to disband. The proposal was overwhelmingly voted down. Stung by the rejection but still proud, Garrison announced he was stepping down as president of the organization he had helped establish thirty-two years earlier. "My vocation, as an Abolitionist, thank God, is ended," he said.[53]

As Garrison had promised, the *Liberator* continued publishing until the end of the year. The country's blacks, including more than three million freed by the war, were losing their most stalwart editorial supporter. With only the *Anti-Slavery Standard* and a few other journals still publishing, the era of the abolitionist press was coming to an end. The growing storm over Reconstruction—and the civil rights of blacks in a newly restored nation—was just beginning. However, that would largely be left to others in the press to face.

EIGHT

◇

CONCLUSION

On December 20, 1865, William Lloyd Garrison tied on his tattered printer's apron and began setting the type for another editorial in the *Liberator*. However, this time the editor was not railing against another outrage. Instead, Garrison was overjoyed at being able to make an "unspeakably cheering" announcement: the Thirteenth Amendment had finally been ratified. Thirty-five years after he founded the *Liberator*—and just a week before it closed—Garrison could announce in the newspaper that the "covenant with death" had been ended by a constitutional amendment. "Hail, redeemed, regenerated America!" Garrison proclaimed with understandable pride. "Hail, North and South, East and West! Hail, the cause of Peace, of Liberty, of Righteousness . . . Hail, ye ransomed millions . . . Hail, all nations, tribes, kindreds and peoples 'made of one blood.'"[1]

It was only fitting that the *Liberator*—and the handful of other abolitionist newspapers still publishing—should announce the ratification of the amendment abolishing slavery. For more than forty years, the publications had helped stir the consciences of Americans and make slavery an issue the United States had to confront. The press was one of the most important tools that abolitionists used in their long struggle to end slavery. Abolitionist newspapers provided a platform for the movement's leaders to spread their views. They publicized the work of anti-slavery societies and helped the societies recruit new members. They printed slave narratives and accounts of runaway slaves. They put on display the devastating impact of slavery and racism. At a time when most newspapers in the North and South were opposed to the antislavery movement—if not supportive of the institution itself—the abolitionist press was the only editorial voice of opposition to slavery for many years.

Antislavery editors supported the pamphlet campaign and the petition drive. They decried the Compromise of 1850 and the Fugitive Slave Law. They seized on the slave power threat as a propaganda device and blamed slave interests for the Kansas-Nebraska Act. They praised the fanatical courage of John Brown and declared him a hero for the abolitionist cause. They had mixed feelings about Abraham Lincoln's historic election but delighted in the South's angry reaction to the event. During the war, they pressed for the Emancipation Proclamation and then for a constitutional amendment to officially end slavery. They also fought for the rights of free blacks to enlist in the military and for black soldiers to receive the same pay as whites. And they did all this with the threat of violence constantly hanging over them.

This is certainly not to say that all the abolitionist press was alike. Antislavery editors disagreed on the goals and tactics of the movement, and more often than not their disputes were played out in the pages of abolitionist publications. Blunt, cantankerous, and hopelessly self-righteous, editors sometimes seemed to spend as much time battling one another as they did battling slavery.

The most influential abolitionist newspapers reflected the views and interests of their editor or sponsoring antislavery society. The *Genius of Universal Emancipation* touted colonization, a passion of Benjamin Lundy. The *Liberator* was the most radical paper and bore the unmistakable stamp of Garrison, including his divisive views on other reform subjects. The *National Anti-Slavery Standard* often followed Garrison's thinking but was far less consistent because it frequently changed editors. The *Philanthropist* and *National Era* were more moderate and mirrored Gamaliel Bailey's interest in politics. The *Anti-Slavery Bugle* reflected the Garrisonian views of the Western Anti-Slavery Society. The *North Star,* the most successful black-owned newspaper, mirrored the radical viewpoint of Frederick Douglass and also devoted considerable attention to issues of importance to free blacks.

But abolitionist newspapers shared the common belief that slavery was, at its core, a national sin, and that a fallen America must redeem itself. As abolitionist strategies and tactics shifted, so did the viewpoints of most of the movement's publications. Early newspapers initially supported the American Colonization Society, but many changed to reflect the new goal of immediate emancipation. Editors encouraged the pamphlet and petitions campaigns, but when it became clear they were not working as hoped, some editors endorsed the move into the political arena. As antislavery opponents used vigilance committees and mob violence to silence the press, editors recognized that the threat to freedom of expression could be successfully exploited. The abolitionist press also relentlessly pushed for both the Emancipation Proclamation and the Thirteenth Amendment, even as others claimed that freeing the slaves should not be the foremost aim of the Civil War.

Certainly, the abolitionist press had its share of problems, from long-winded editorials and overly sentimental poetry to sloppy editing and erratic production. Most publications were started with insufficient capital, and all had to depend on the financial support of antislavery societies, the goodwill of generous benefactors, or, in some cases, both. Even then, many newspapers closed after publishing for just a year or two. With their radical viewpoints, abolitionist journals could never expect to attract large numbers of readers. But there also were simply too many antislavery publications, given the small size of the audience.

The fact that so many abolitionist publications were started, despite the great odds of failure, was due in large part to the widely held belief at the time that the press had a significant influence on public opinion. Nineteenth-century editors believed passionately in the power of the printed word. Moreover, they maintained that a free press was one of the surest safeguards of a democratic government and, in a democracy, citizens must be properly informed. Abolitionist editors were convinced that honest, intelligent people, if shown the unmistakable evils of slavery, would eventually force the government to end the institution. That is why abolitionist editors believed in the liberty of the press, and why they spoke so zealously about their right to criticize the government, even while others complained they wanted to overturn the country.

After the Civil War, most abolitionist editors recognized that the victory they had worked to achieve was ambiguous at best. Although slavery was legally dead, racism remained stubbornly steadfast. The Fifteenth Amendment, which prohibited both federal and state governments from denying or abridging the right to vote "on account of race, color, or previous condition of servitude," finally passed Congress in 1869. Ratification of the amendment allowed the American Anti-Slavery Society to declare its mission completed, and the society disbanded the following year. Radical Republicans soon fractured into competing interests, and in 1876 federal troops were removed from the South, effectively ending Reconstruction. Democratic "redeemer" governments returned to power in the old Confederate states and turned a blind eye to groups such as the Ku Klux Klan, which used violence to terrorize former slaves. Tragically, the violence and intimidation, not to mention widespread discrimination and segregation, continued for many decades. Far more than antislavery editorial rhetoric would be needed to transform American racial attitudes.

However, this should not diminish the achievements of abolitionist newspapers. Never before, and perhaps never since, had the reform press in this country tackled a subject of such significance with such tenacity over an extended period—all the while facing enormous public criticism and hostility. Antislavery editors were an unfailing voice of outrage for decades. Fueled by evangelical religious zeal, they provided a collective editorial vision, constantly reminding Americans of the freedoms guaranteed by the Constitution and demanding that they be honored for all people, no matter their color. Branded as wild-eyed and dangerous fanatics, the editors thrived on the controversy they provoked, secure in the belief that they were absolutely right.

Although antislavery journalism largely came to an end after the war, its legacy continued to be felt well into the twentieth century. The abolitionist press became a model for the advocacy press that would go hand in hand with later reform causes in the United States, including the women's suffrage movement and the civil rights movement. Although antislavery editors such as Garrison, Lundy, Bailey, Douglass, and others did not pioneer the techniques of reform journalism, they took them to a higher level. Abolitionist newspapers showed what could be accomplished by consistent and unyielding commitment to a cause. In so doing, they helped America finally begin to realize the full promise of its Constitution.

NOTES

PREFACE

1. Quoted in Merton L. Dillon, *Benjamin Lundy and the Struggle for Negro Freedom* (Urbana: University of Illinois Press, 1966), 141; *Freedom's Journal,* March 16, 1827; *Philanthropist,* October 7, 1836.

2. *Emancipator,* October 8, 1845.

3. *Genius of Universal Emancipation,* October 1821.

CHAPTER ONE

1. *Philanthropist,* June 2, 1821.

2. Asa E. Martin, "Pioneer Anti-Slavery Press," *Mississippi Valley Historical Review* 2 (1925): 509–28.

3. For background on Lundy, this chapter relies upon Dillon, *Benjamin Lundy;* and Thomas Earle, ed., *The Life, Travels and Opinions of Benjamin Lundy* (Philadelphia, 1847).

4. Martin, "Pioneer Anti-Slavery Press," 514–20.

5. *Emancipator,* April 30, 1820; Merton Dillon, *Slavery Attacked: Southern Slaves and Their Allies* (Baton Rouge: Louisiana State University Press, 1990), 119–27.

6. Dillon, *Benjamin Lundy,* 46–47.

7. *Genius,* January 1822; *Genius,* June 1823.

8. David Brion Davis, "The Emergence of Immediatism in British and American Antislavery Thought," *Mississippi Valley Historical Review* 49 (September 1962): 213–14.

9. *Genius,* September 1821; *Genius,* January 1822; *Genius,* September 1822.

10. *Genius,* March 1822; *Genius,* November 1821.

11. *Genius*, October 16, 1829; *Genius*, March 5, 1830.

12. Dillon, *Benjamin Lundy*, 48–51.

13. *Genius*, June 1824; Earle, *Life of Benjamin Lundy*, 20–22.

14. James Brewer Stewart, *Holy Warriors: The Abolitionists and American Slavery* (New York: Hill and Wang, 1976), 29–32; Leon F. Litwack, *North of Slavery: The Negro in the Free States, 1790–1860* (Chicago: University of Chicago Press, 1961), 20–29.

15. *Genius*, October 1824.

16. Earle, *Life of Benjamin Lundy*, 23–24; Dillon, *Benjamin Lundy*, 88–103.

17. Dillon, *Benjamin Lundy*, 117–20; *Genius*, January 2, 1827.

18. *Genius*, January 2, 1827.

19. Jacqueline Bacon, *Freedom's Journal: The First African-American Newspaper* (Lanham, Md.: Lexington Books, 2007); Carter R. Bryan, "Negro Journalism in America Before Emancipation," *Journalism Monographs* 12 (September 1969): 1–15; Bernell Tripp, *Origins of the Black Press: New York, 1827–1847* (Northport, Ala.: Vision, 1992), 12–29; *Freedom's Journal*, March 16, 1827.

20. *Freedom's Journal*, March 16, 1827.

21. Kenneth D. Nordin, "In Search of Black Unity: An Interpretation of the Content and Function of *Freedom's Journal*," *Journalism History* 4 (Winter 1977): 123–28.

22. *Freedom's Journal*, June 8, 1827.

23. *Freedom's Journal*, March 16, 1827.

24. *Freedom's Journal*, October 5, 1827.

25. Quoted in Bacon, *Freedom's Journal*, 105–6, 61–62.

26. Bacon, *Freedom's Journal*, 59–64; Bryan, "Negro Journalism," 8–10; *Freedom's Journal*, September 7, 1827; *Freedom's Journal*, March 14, 1829.

27. *Rights of All*, May 29, 1829; *Rights of All*, June 12, 1829; *Rights of All*, September 18, 1829.

28. *Liberator*, September 20, 1839. For background on Garrison, this chapter relies upon John L. Thomas, *The Liberator: William Lloyd Garrison* (Boston: Little, Brown, 1963); and Henry Mayer, *All on Fire: William Lloyd Garrison and the Abolition of Slavery* (New York: St. Martin's Griffin, 1998).

29. Thomas, *The Liberator*, 7–73; Mayer, *All on Fire*, 9–51.

30. *National Philanthropist*, March 21, 1828.

31. *Genius*, September 2, 1829.

32. *Genius*, September 2, 1829; Paul Goodman, *Of One Blood: Abolitionism and the Origins of Racial Equality* (Berkeley and Los Angeles: University of California Press, 1998), 36–44.

33. *Genius*, October 16, 1829.

34. *Genius*, November 20, 1829; Thomas, *The Liberator*, 108–10.

35. Thomas, *The Liberator*, 111–13.

36. Dillon, *Benjamin Lundy*, 158–59.

37. Quoted in Thomas, *The Liberator*, 126–27.

38. Quoted in Mayer, *All on Fire*, 110.

39. *Genius*, November 27, 1829; *Liberator*, January 1, 1831; Mayer, *All on Fire*, 106–13.

40. *Liberator*, January 8, 1831; *Liberator*, January 15, 1831; Mayer, *All on Fire*, 114–15.

41. Rodger Streitmatter, *Raising Her Voice: African-American Women Journalists Who Changed History* (Lexington: University of Kentucky Press, 1994), 15–24.

42. William E. Huntzicker, *The Popular Press, 1833–1865* (Westport, Conn.: Greenwood, 1999).

43. Thomas, *The Liberator*, 131–32.

44. Merton Dillon, *Slavery Attacked: Southern Slaves and Their Allies* (Baton Rouge: Louisiana State University Press, 1990), 145–50; *Liberator*, January 8, 1831.

45. Louis Filler, *The Crusade Against Slavery, 1830–1860* (New York: Harper and Row, 1960), 52–54; *Liberator*, September 3, 1831.

46. *Liberator*, September 10, 1831; *National Intelligencer*, September 15, 1831; *National Intelligencer*, September 30, 1831.

47. *Liberator*, September 10, 1831; *Liberator*, September 17, 1831; *Liberator*, September 24, 1831.

48. Thomas, *The Liberator*, 135–38.

49. *Liberator*, October 22, 1831; Mayer, *All on Fire*, 118–23; Thomas, *The Liberator*, 138–39.

50. *Genius*, October 1831; Earle, *Life of Benjamin Lundy*, 28–31; Dillon, *Benjamin Lundy*, 165–67.

51. Dillon, *Benjamin Lundy*, 170.

52. *Genius*, March 1832; *Genius*, April 1832.

53. Dillon, *Benjamin Lundy*, 176–78.

54. *Genius*, November 1832.

CHAPTER TWO

1. *Liberator*, January 1, 1832.

2. Quoted in Carolyn Karcher, *The First Woman in the Republic: A Cultural Biography of Lydia Maria Child* (Durham, N.C.: Duke University Press, 1994), 175.

3. Davis, "Emergence of Immediatism," 209–30; *Liberator*, March 26, 1830.

4. Mayer, *All on Fire*, 127–31; Thomas, *The Liberator*, 139–43; *Liberator*, February 18, 1832.

5. *Liberator*, July 9, 1831; Mayer, *All on Fire*, 133–39.

6. Quoted in Dillon, *Benjamin Lundy*, 246–47.

7. Quoted in Mayer, *All on Fire*, 118–19; Filler, *Crusade Against Slavery*, 48–52.

8. Mayer, *All on Fire*, 166–68; Thomas, *The Liberator*, 167–69.

9. *Liberator*, October 12, 1833.

10. Louis Ruchames, ed., *The Abolitionists: A Collection of Their Writings* (New York: Capricorn Books, 1963), 78–83; Stewart, *Holy Warriors*, 50–55; Mayer, *All on Fire*, 173–77; *Liberator*, December 14, 1833.

11. Stewart, *Holy Warriors*, 42–55; Filler, *Crusade Against Slavery*, 28–47.

12. Bertram Wyatt-Brown, "The Abolitionists' Postal Campaign of 1835," *Journal of Negro History* 50 (October 1965): 227–38.

13. David Paul Nord, "The Evangelical Origins of Mass Media in America, 1815–1835," *Journalism Monographs* 88 (May 1984): 1–30; Leonard L. Richards, *"Gentlemen of Property and Standing": Anti-Abolition Mobs in Jacksonian America* (New York: Oxford University Press, 1970), 71–73, 149–63; John Nerone, *Violence Against the Press: Policing the Public Sphere in U. S. History* (New York: Oxford University Press, 1994), 87–90.

14. Russel B. Nye, *Fettered Freedom: Civil Liberties and the Slavery Controversy, 1830–1860* (East Lansing: Michigan State University Press, 1963), 67–72; Richards, *"Gentlemen of Property and Standing,"* 54–55.

15. Wyatt-Brown, "Abolitionists' Postal Campaign," 229–31.

16. *Liberator*, August 15, 1835; Clement Eaton, *Freedom of Thought in the Old South* (Durham, N.C.: Duke University Press, 1940), 126–29.

17. Quoted in Nye, *Fettered Freedom*, 69–70.

18. Nye, *Fettered Freedom*, 70–75.

19. Nye, *Fettered Freedom*, 175–76.

20. *Philanthropist*, February 26, 1836; *Philanthropist*, July 15, 1836; *Philanthropist*, March 25, 1836; *Liberator*, August 6, 1836.

21. Nye, *Fettered Freedom*, 41–85; *Liberator*, April 2, 1836; *Philanthropist*, January 15, 1836.

22. Hugh Davis, *Joshua Leavitt, Evangelical Abolitionist* (Baton Rouge: Louisiana State University Press, 1990), 1–33.

23. I. Garland Penn, *The Afro-American Press and Its Editors* (New York: Arno, 1969), 32–57.

24. *Colored American*, March 4, 1837; *Colored American*, May 6, 1837; *Colored American*, September 30, 1837.

25. *Colored American*, January 1, 1837; *Colored American*, April 22, 1837.

26. *Colored American*, March 4, 1837; *Colored American*, September 30, 1837.

27. *Colored American*, May 27, 1837; *Colored American*, July 15, 1837.

28. *Colored American*, May 3, 1838; Litwack, *North of Slavery*, 240.

29. Nerone, *Violence Against the Press*, 84–110.

30. Dillon, *The Abolitionists*, 100–103.

31. Nye, *Fettered Freedom*, 44–45.

32. Gilbert Hobbs Barnes, *The Antislavery Impulse, 1830–1844* (New York: Harcourt, Brace and World, 1964), 130–37; *Philanthropist*, December 2, 1836.

33. *Liberator*, February 11, 1837; *Emancipator*, December 16, 1834; *Philanthropist*, December 23, 1836.

34. Nye, *Fettered Freedom*, 48–66.

35. *Philanthropist,* July 1, 1836; *Liberator,* February 13, 1836; *Liberator,* March 11, 1837.

36. *Liberator,* November 8, 1834.

CHAPTER THREE

1. *Philanthropist,* July 15, 1836.

2. *Philanthropist,* July 22, 1836.

3. Nerone, *Violence Against the Press,* 84–110. In his study, Nerone counted a total of 134 cases of violence directed at abolitionists. Twenty-four of these were directed against the press, either at an editor or the newspaper itself.

4. Richards, *"Gentlemen of Property and Standing,"* 30–35; Litwack, *North of Slavery,* 30–213.

5. Michael Feldberg, *The Turbulent Era: Riot and Disorder in Jacksonian America* (New York: Oxford University Press, 1980); Stewart, *Holy Warriors,* 64–68; David Grimstead, "Rioting in Its Jacksonian Setting," *American Historical Review* 77 (April 1972): 361–97.

6. Richard B. Kielbowicz, "The Law and Mob Law in Attacks on Antislavery Newspapers, 1833–1860," *Law and History Review* 24 (Fall 2006): 559–600; Michael Kent Curtis, *Free Speech, "The People's Darling Privilege": Struggles for Freedom of Expression in American History* (Durham, N.C.: Duke University Press, 2000).

7. Richards, *"Gentlemen of Property and Standing,"* 82–130.

8. Thomas, *The Liberator,* 184; Richards, *"Gentlemen of Property and Standing,"* 17.

9. *Liberator,* August 15, 1835; *Anti-Slavery Record* quoted in Nye, *Fettered Freedom,* 197–98.

10. *National Anti-Slavery Standard,* September 8, 1842; *Anti-Slavery Standard,* July 5, 1856.

11. Whittier and Garrison, quoted in Stewart, *Holy Warriors,* 73.

12. Thomas, *The Liberator,* 199–204; Mayer, *All on Fire,* 199–206.

13. *Liberator,* October 24, 1835.

14. Thomas, *The Liberator,* 199–204; Mayer, *All on Fire,* 199–206.

15. Newspaper quotes from Mayer, *All on Fire,* 206–7.

16. *Liberator,* November 14, 1835; Nerone, *Violence Against the Press,* 100; *Anti-Slavery Standard,* September 8, 1842.

17. For background on Birney, this chapter relies upon Betty Fladeland, *James Gillespie Birney: Slaveholder to Abolitionist* (Ithaca, N.Y.: Cornell University Press, 1955); and William Birney, *James G. Birney and His Times* (New York: Appleton, 1890).

18. John Nerone, *The Culture of the Press in the Early Republic: Cincinnati, 1793–1848* (New York: Garland, 1989), 262–63.

19. *Philanthropist,* January 1, 1836.

20. *Philanthropist,* January 29, 1836.

21. Quoted in Fladeland, *James Gillespie Birney,* 133–34.

22. *Philanthropist,* July 22, 1836; Fladeland, *James Gillespie Birney,* 136–38.

23. *Philanthropist,* July 29, 1836.

24. *Philanthropist,* August 5, 1836; Fladeland, *James Gillespie Birney,* 139–42.

25. *Philanthropist,* October 21, 1836.

26. Fladeland, *James Gillespie Birney,* 144–47, 154–60.

27. For background on Lovejoy, this chapter relies upon Merton L. Dillon, *Elijah P. Lovejoy, Abolitionist Editor* (Urbana: University of Illinois Press, 1961).

28. *St. Louis Observer,* November 22, 1833.

29. Dillon, *Elijah P. Lovejoy,* 48–50, 54–56; *St. Louis Observer,* May 15, 1834.

30. *St. Louis Observer,* November 5, 1835.

31. *St. Louis Observer,* February 11, 1836; May 5, 1836; June 2, 1836; Dillon, *Elijah P. Lovejoy,* 75–88.

32. *St. Louis Observer—Extra,* August 10, 1836; *Alton Observer,* September 8, 1836.

33. Dillon, *Elijah P. Lovejoy,* 94–115.

34. *Alton Telegraph,* September 27, 1837.

35. Dillon, *Elijah P. Lovejoy,* 159–70.

36. *Emancipator,* November 7, 1837; *Philanthropist,* November 21, 1837; *Colored American,* November 25, 1837. *New Hampshire Statesman* and *Boston Times* quoted in *Emancipator,* November 7, 1837.

37. *Genius,* December 1836; Dillon, *Benjamin Lundy,* 235–36.

38. *National Enquirer,* March 8, 1838; Dillon, *Benjamin Lundy,* 251–53.

39. *Pennsylvania Freeman,* May 17, 1838; Earle, *Life of Benjamin Lundy,* 299–303; Dillon, *Benjamin Lundy,* 253–62; John A. Pollard, *John Greenleaf Whittier, Friend of Man* (Boston: Houghton Mifflin, 1949), 162–65.

40. *Genius,* 1823; *Liberator,* September 20, 1839.

CHAPTER FOUR

1. Mayer, *All on Fire,* 234.

2. Thomas, *The Liberator,* 242–44.

3. Ronald G. Walters, *The Antislavery Appeal: American Abolitionism After 1830* (Baltimore: Johns Hopkins University Press), 3–18.

4. *Liberator,* January 1, 1838.

5. *Liberator,* October 12, 1838; Mayer, *All on Fire,* 250–51.

6. *Liberator,* October 26, 1838; *Liberator,* December 7, 1838.

7. *Liberator,* October 26, 1838; *Liberator,* December 7, 1838.

8. Thomas, *The Liberator,* 224–27.

9. *Emancipator,* October 18, 1838; *Genius,* June 28, 1839; Stanley Harrold, *Gamaliel Bailey and Antislavery Union* (Kent, Ohio: Kent State University Press, 1986), 21–23.

10. Filler, *Crusade Against Slavery,* 129–35; *Liberator,* January 11, 1839.

11. *Liberator,* February 1, 1839; *Massachusetts Abolitionist* quoted in Mayer, *All on Fire,* 258.

12. *Liberator,* February 14, 1840.

13. *Liberator,* April 3, 1840; *Emancipator,* April 16, 1840.

14. Quoted in Walter Merrill, *Against Wind and Tide: A Biography of William Lloyd Garrison* (Cambridge, Mass.: Harvard University Press, 1963), 156.

15. *Liberator,* April 10, 1840; *Liberator,* April 17, 1840.

16. Thomas, *The Liberator,* 289–93; Mayer, *All on Fire,* 276–84.

17. Garrison quoted in Thomas, *The Liberator,* 292.

18. *Anti-Slavery Standard,* June 11, 1840; *Anti-Slavery Standard,* June 18, 1840.

19. Filler, *Crusade Against Slavery,* 150–53; Fladeland, *James Gillespie Birney,* 179–89.

20. *Anti-Slavery Standard,* June 24, 1841; *Emancipator,* October 10, 1839; *Emancipator,* October 17, 1839; Davis, *Joshua Leavitt,* 152–53.

21. *Liberator,* January 3, 1840; *Liberator,* March 13, 1840.

22. *Liberator,* April 10, 1840; Goodell quoted in Thomas, *The Liberator,* 287.

23. Davis, *Joshua Leavitt,* 164–67.

24. Harrold, *Gamaliel Bailey,* 30–35; *Philanthropist,* May 5, 1840.

25. *Emancipator,* November 12, 1840; *Philanthropist,* November 18, 1840.

26. *Liberator,* October 23, 1840; *Liberator,* October 30, 1840; *Liberator,* November 13, 1840.

27. *Liberator,* January 1, 1840; *Liberator,* April 16, 1840.

28. *Liberator,* September 16, 1842; *Liberator,* March 13, 1846.

29. For background on Bailey, this chapter relies upon Harrold, *Gamaliel Bailey,* 1–18.

30. Harrold, *Gamaliel Bailey,* 41–43.

31. *Philanthropist,* October 6, 1841; Harrold, *Gamaliel Bailey,* 42–44; Richards, *"Gentlemen of Property and Standing,"* 40–43.

32. Harrold, *Gamaliel Bailey,* 43–45.

33. *Anti-Slavery Bugle,* June 20, 1845; *Anti-Slavery Bugle,* June 25, 1847; *Anti-Slavery Bugle,* July 16, 1847.

34. Davis, *Joshua Leavitt,* 167–68, 185–86.

35. Quoted in Thomas, *The Liberator,* 338.

36. Quoted in Karcher, *First Woman in the Republic,* 269–70.

37. Karcher, *First Woman in the Republic,* 273–76.

38. *Anti-Slavery Standard,* May 4, 1843.

39. Thomas, *The Liberator,* 338–39.

40. *Liberator,* November 26, 1841; *Liberator,* April 22, 1842.

41. *Liberator,* February 3, 1843; *Liberator,* May 24, 1844.

42. Mayer, *All on Fire,* 314; Harrold, *Gamaliel Bailey,* 72; Aileen S. Kraditor, *Ends and Means in American Abolitionism: Garrison and His Critics on Strategy and Tactics, 1834–1850* (New York: Pantheon Books, 1967), 200.

43. *Liberator,* May 24, 1844.

44. *Liberator,* August 12, 1842.

CHAPTER FIVE

1. *Philanthropist,* March 6, 1844.

2. Harrold, *Gamaliel Bailey,* 81–84; Barnes, *Antislavery Impulse,* 177–90; Bertram Wyatt-Brown, *Lewis Tappan and the Evangelical War Against Slavery* (Cleveland: Press of Case Western Reserve University), 1969.

3. Harrold, *Gamaliel Bailey,* 81–84.

4. *National Era,* January 7, 1847.

5. Harrold, *Gamaliel Bailey,* 87–88.

6. *National Era,* March 1, 1850.

7. Harrold, *Gamaliel Bailey,* 106–8.

8. Harrold, *Gamaliel Bailey,* 88–89; *National Era,* February 18, 1847.

9. *National Era,* June 20, 1850; Harrold, *Gamaliel Bailey,* 90–91.

10. Harrold, *Gamaliel Bailey,* 139–41.

11. *Anti-Slavery Bugle,* January 29, 1847; *National Era,* July 22, 1847; *National Era,* February 25, 1847; *National Era,* May 20, 1847.

12. Davis, *Joshua Leavitt,* 235–37.

13. *National Era,* April 20, 1848; *National Era,* April 27, 1848; Harrold, *Gamaliel Bailey,* 125–27.

14. David M. Potter, *The Impending Crisis, 1848–1861* (New York: Harper and Row, 1976), 1–17; Dillon, *Slavery Attacked,* 217–23.

15. *Liberator,* March 7, 1846; *Anti-Slavery Bugle,* March 10, 1847.

16. *Liberator,* May 7, 1847; *National Era,* June 3, 1847; *Emancipator,* January 13, 1847; *Emancipator,* January 27, 1847; *Emancipator,* May 26, 1847.

17. Willard B. Gatewood Jr., ed., *Free Man of Color: The Autobiography of Willis Augustus Hodges* (Knoxville: University of Tennessee Press, 1982), 76–77.

18. *Ram's Horn,* January 1, 1847; Tripp, *Origins of the Black Press,* 44–56.

19. Editorial quoted in Tripp, *Origins of the Black Press,* 50.

20. For background on Douglass, this chapter relies upon Frederick Douglass, *My Bondage and My Freedom* (New York: Penguin, 2003); and Benjamin Quarles, *Frederick Douglass* (New York: Associated Publishers, 1948).

21. Philip S. Foner, ed., *The Life and Writings of Frederick Douglass,* vol. 1 (New York: International Publishers, 1950), 48.

22. *Liberator,* October 13, 1843; Douglass quoted in Quarles, *Frederick Douglass,* 15.

23. *Liberator,* July 23, 1847; Douglass, *My Bondage and My Freedom,* 290.

24. Quoted in Foner, *The Life and Writings of Frederick Douglass,* 75–83.

25. Douglass, *My Bondage and My Freedom,* 291.

26. *North Star,* December 3, 1847; *North Star,* May 4, 1849.

27. *North Star,* May 4, 1849.

28. *North Star,* July 14, 1848; *North Star,* July 21, 1848.

29. *North Star,* September 22, 1848; The letter to Auld was reprinted as an appendix in *My Bondage and My Freedom.*

30. *Liberator,* May 5, 1848.

31. Richard H. Sewell, *Ballots for Freedom: Antislavery Politics in the United States, 1837–1860* (New York: Oxford University Press, 1976), 152–65.

32. *North Star,* August 11, 1848; *Emancipator,* August 16, 1848; *Emancipator,* September 13, 1848; Garrison quoted in Thomas, *The Liberator,* 355–56.

33. Jane Grey Swisshelm, *Half a Century* (Chicago: Jansen, McClurg, 1880), 51–59, 105–23; Kathleen L. Endres, "Jane Grey Swisshelm: 19th Century Journalist and Feminist," *Journalism History* 2 (Winter 1975): 128–32.

34. *Pittsburgh Saturday Visiter,* November 23, 1850.

35. *Pittsburgh Saturday Visiter,* August 19, 1848.

36. *North Star,* May 25, 1849.

37. *Liberator,* November 10, 1848; *Liberator,* January 12, 1849.

38. Potter, *Impending Crisis,* 90–120.

39. *Liberator,* July 1, 1850; *North Star,* July 1, 1850.

40. Quoted in Harrold, *Gamaliel Bailey,* 131–32.

41. *National Era,* May 2, 1850; *Liberator,* July 26, 1850.

42. Potter, *Impending Crisis,* 90–120.

43. *National Era,* December 5, 1850.

CHAPTER SIX

1. Harrold, *Gamaliel Bailey*, 142–44; Thomas F. Gossett, *"Uncle Tom's Cabin" and American Literature* (Dallas: Southern Methodist University Press, 1985), 166.

2. Nye, *Fettered Freedom*, 257–58.

3. Nye, *Fettered Freedom*, 260–64; *Anti-Slavery Standard*, January 16, 1845.

4. *Pennsylvania Freeman*, September 19, 1850; *Anti-Slavery Standard*, August 28, 1851.

5. *Anti-Slavery Bugle*, October 11, 1851; *Anti-Slavery Bugle*, November 8, 1851.

6. *Anti-Slavery Bugle*, September 15, 1851.

7. Quarles, *Frederick Douglass*, 117–19.

8. Stanley W. Campbell, *The Slave Catchers: Enforcement of the Fugitive Slave Law, 1850–1860* (Chapel Hill: University of North Carolina Press, 1968), 151–54; *Liberator*, September 26, 1851; *National Era*, October 23, 1851.

9. Campbell, *Slave Catchers*, 124–32; *Liberator*, June 9, 1854; *National Era*, June 8, 1854.

10. Mayer, *All on Fire*, 440–44; *Liberator*, July 14, 1854; *Liberator*, July 21, 1854.

11. *Philanthropist*, June 7, 1837; *Anti-Slavery Bugle*, December 4, 1852.

12. *National Era*, May 21, 1857; *Anti-Slavery Bugle*, November 9, 1850.

13. Nye, *Fettered Freedom*, 300.

14. Quoted in Nye, *Fettered Freedom*, 100.

15. Quarles, *Frederick Douglass*, 73–79; Mayer, *All on Fire*, 428–33.

16. *Liberator*, November 14, 1851.

17. Quarles, *Frederick Douglass*, 73–79; Mayer, *All on Fire*, 428–33.

18. Potter, *Impending Crisis*, 145–76.

19. *Frederick Douglass' Paper*, February 24, 1854.

20. Harrold, *Gamaliel Bailey*, 159; Potter, *Impending Crisis*, 162–64; Sewell, *Ballots for Freedom*, 254–56; *National Era*, January 24, 1854.

21. Quoted in Glyndon G. Van Deusen, *Horace Greeley: Nineteenth-Century Crusader* (New York: Hill and Wang, 1953), 180.

22. Harrold, *Gamaliel Bailey,* 160–66; Eric Foner, *Free Soil, Free Labor, Free Men: The Ideology of the Republican Party Before the Civil War* (New York: Oxford University Press, 1970), 115–33.

23. Sewell, *Ballots for Freedom,* 254–91.

24. *National Era,* April 19, 1855; *National Era,* May 3, 1855; *Liberator,* November 10, 1854; *Liberator,* November 17, 1854.

25. *Frederick Douglass' Paper,* April 25, 1856; *Frederick Douglass' Paper,* June 10, 1856.

26. James A. Rawley, *Race and Politics: "Bleeding Kansas" and the Coming of the Civil War* (Philadelphia: J. B. Lippincott, 1969), 129–34.

27. Potter, *Impending Crisis,* 199–224; James M. McPherson, *Battle Cry of Freedom: The Civil War Era* (New York: Oxford University Press, 1988), 145–69.

28. *National Era,* May 22, 1856; *National Era,* June 12, 1856; *National Era,* July 10, 1856; *Evening Journal* and *Evening Post* quoted in Ratner and Teeter, *Fanatics and Fire-Eaters,* 39.

29. Harrold, *Gamaliel Bailey,* 180–82; *National Era,* October 23, 1856.

30. Quarles, *Frederick Douglass,* 161–162; *Frederick Douglass' Paper,* August 15, 1856.

31. Thomas, *Liberator,* 388–89.

32. Harrold, *Gamaliel Bailey,* 180–82.

33. Potter, *Impending Crisis,* 267–96; McPherson, *Battle Cry of Freedom,* 170–81.

34. *Anti-Slavery Bugle,* March 1, 1850.

35. *Anti-Slavery Bugle,* March 20, 1857; *National Era,* March 26, 1857; *National Era,* April 2, 1857; *Independent,* April 18, 1857.

36. Quoted in Lorman A. Ratner and Dwight L. Teeter Jr., *Fanatics and Fire-Eaters: Newspapers and the Coming of the Civil War* (Urbana: University of Illinois Press, 2003), 54–55; Potter, *Impending Crisis,* 281.

37. Louis M. Starr, *The Bohemian Brigade: Civil War Newsmen in Action* (New York: Knopf, 1954), 18–19, 98–99.

38. Quoted in Harrold, *Gamaliel Bailey,* 185.

39. Harrold, *Gamaliel Bailey,* 186–88, 211–13.

40. *Liberator,* June 24, 1859.

41. Stephen B. Oates, *To Purge This Land with Blood: A Biography of John Brown* (New York, 1970).

42. McPherson, *Battle Cry of Freedom,* 202–13.

43. C. Vann Woodward, *The Burden of Southern History* (Baton Rouge: Louisiana State University Press, 1960), 41–68; *Anti-Slavery Standard,* December 10, 1859.

44. *Liberator,* November 1, 1858; *Liberator,* November 30, 1858.

45. Ratner and Teeter, *Fanatics and Fire-Eaters,* 80–83.

46. *Douglass' Monthly,* November 1859; Quarles, *Frederick Douglass,* 169–85; *Douglass' Monthly,* December 1860.

47. William Gienapp, ed., *This Fiery Trial: The Speeches and Writings of Abraham Lincoln* (New York: Oxford University Press, 2002), 58–60, 43–51.

48. *Douglass' Monthly,* June 1860; *Anti-Slavery Standard,* June 2, 1860.

49. Quoted in Thomas, *The Liberator,* 398–400.

50. *Anti-Slavery Standard,* November 24, 1860; *Douglass' Monthly,* December 1860; *Independent,* November 8, 1860.

51. Donald E. Reynolds, *Editors Make War: Southern Newspapers in the Secession Crisis* (Nashville, Tenn.: Vanderbilt University Press, 1966), 139–60; *Liberator,* November 16, 1860; *Liberator,* January 14, 1861.

CHAPTER SEVEN

1. *Liberator,* June 7, 1861; Mayer, *All on Fire,* 518–19.

2. *Douglass' Monthly,* January 1861.

3. *Daily Post* quoted in Ratner and Teeter, *Fanatics and Fire-Eaters,* 103–4.

4. James M. McPherson, *Struggle for Equality: Abolitionists and the Negro in the Civil War and Reconstruction* (Princeton, N.J.: Princeton University Press, 1964), 40–45.

5. *Liberator,* December 7, 1861; *Liberator,* December 14, 1861; *Douglass' Monthly,* January 1861; *Anti-Slavery Standard,* March 2, 1861.

6. *Douglass' Monthly,* April 1861.

7. McPherson, *Struggle for Equality,* 40–45; *Douglass' Monthly,* May 1861; *Liberator,* April 26, 1861. For a discussion of Garrison's change in views, see Mayer, *All on Fire,* 519–21.

8. McPherson, *Struggle for Equality,* 46–48; *Anti-Slavery Standard,* April 20, 1861; *Anti-Slavery Standard,* April 27, 1861; *Anglo-African,* May 11, 1861.

9. *Anti-Slavery Standard,* April 27, 1861; *Douglass' Monthly,* October 1861.

10. *Liberator,* July 12, 1861.

11. *Philadelphia Inquirer,* July 25, 1861.

12. *Douglass' Monthly,* July 1861; *Douglass' Monthly,* August 1861; *Douglass' Monthly,* September 1861.

13. *Anti-Slavery Standard,* September 28, 1861; *Liberator,* December 6, 1861; *Douglass' Monthly,* October 1861.

14. Frank Luther Mott, *A History of American Magazines, Volume II: 1850–1865* (Cambridge, Mass.: Harvard University Press, 1938), 367–73; Louis Filler, "Liberalism, Anti-Slavery, and the Founders of the *Independent,*" *New England Quarterly* 27 (September 1954): 291–306.

15. Mayer, *All on Fire,* 531.

16. McPherson, *Battle Cry of Freedom,* 494–49; *Principia,* December 21, 1861.

17. *Douglass' Monthly,* February 1862; *Liberator,* December 6, 1861.

18. McPherson, *Struggle for Equality,* 102–3.

19. *Liberator,* July 25, 1862.

20. *New York Tribune,* August 20, 1862; *National Intelligencer,* August 23, 1862. For a discussion of the Greeley-Lincoln exchange, see Allen C. Guelzo, *Lincoln's Emancipation Proclamation: The End of Slavery in America* (New York: Simon and Schuster, 2004), 130–37.

21. *Anti-Slavery Standard,* August 30, 1862.

22. Gienapp, *This Fiery Trial,* 136–37.

23. *Douglass' Monthly,* October 1862; *New York Tribune,* September 23, 1862; *Independent,* September 25, 1862; *Chicago Tribune,* September 23, 1862; *Liberator,* September 26, 1862.

24. Mayer, *All on Fire*, 544–47; Thomas, *The Liberator*, 419–20; *Liberator*, January 9, 1863; *Liberator*, January 16, 1863.

25. *Independent*, June 25, 1863. Some of the information in this section comes from McPherson, *Struggle for Equality*, 221–37.

26. *New York Tribune*, February 4, 1864; *Liberator*, March 20, 1863.

27. *New York Tribune*, July 14, 1863; *Liberator*, July 17, 1863.

28. *Douglass' Monthly*, May 1861; Dudley Taylor Cornish, *The Sable Arm: Negro Troops in the Union Army, 1861–1865* (New York: W. W. Norton, 1966).

29. *Douglass' Monthly*, September 5, 1861.

30. Cornish, *Sable Arm*, 132–42.

31. *Douglass' Monthly*, March 1863.

32. Cornish, *Sable Arm*, 142–56; William S. McFeely, *Frederick Douglass* (New York: W. W. Norton, 1991), 217–27; *Anti-Slavery Standard*, August 8, 1863; *New York Tribune*, September 8, 1865.

33. Cornish, *Sable Arm*, 181–96.

34. *Chicago Tribune*, May 1, 1864; *Anglo-African*, April 30, 1864.

35. *Douglass' Monthly*, August 1863.

36. *Liberator*, February 5, 1864.

37. *Anti-Slavery Standard*, February 13, 1864; *Liberator*, February 26, 1864.

38. *Liberator*, March 18, 1864; Mayer, *All on Fire*, 564–65.

39. McPherson, *Struggle for Equality*, 266–67; Mayer, *All on Fire*, 565–66.

40. *Liberator*, June 24, 1864.

41. *Independent*, June 23, 1864; *Independent*, June 30, 1864.

42. *Philadelphia Inquirer*, June 9, 1864; *New York Tribune*, September 6, 1864; McPherson, *Struggle For Equality*, 283; Van Deusen, *Horace Greeley*, 311.

43. *Liberator*, July 22, 1864.

44. Gienapp, *This Fiery Trial*, 220–21; *National Intelligencer*, March 6, 1865.

45. Guelzo, *Lincoln's Emancipation Proclamation*, 229–32; McPherson, *Battle Cry of Freedom*, 838–40; *Liberator*, February 3, 1865; *New York Times*, February 1, 1865.

46. *Liberator*, December 2, 1864.

47. *Independent,* December 17, 1863; *Anti-Slavery Standard,* December 19, 1863.

48. Robert F. Durden, *The Gray and the Black: The Confederate Debate on Emancipation* (Baton Rouge: Louisiana State University Press, 1972); *Philadelphia Inquirer,* November 11, 1864.

49. *New York Tribune,* February 15, 1865.

50. Edward Chase Kirkland, *The Peacemakers of 1864* (New York: Macmillan, 1927), 197–251; *Liberator,* February 14, 1865.

51. *Liberator,* March 17, 1865; *Liberator,* April 28, 1865; *Liberator,* May 5, 1865; Mayer, *All on Fire,* 580–82.

52. *Liberator,* April 21, 1865; *Independent,* April 20, 1865; *Independent,* April 27, 1865.

53. *Liberator,* May 19, 1865; *Liberator,* May 22, 1865; *Liberator,* June 6, 1865; Thomas, *The Liberator,* 431–35; Mayer, *All on Fire,* 586–94; McPherson, *Struggle for Equality,* 301–7.

CHAPTER EIGHT

1. *Liberator,* December 22, 1865.

BIBLIOGRAPHY

NEWSPAPERS

Anglo-African
Anti-Slavery Bugle
Chicago Tribune
Colored American
Douglass' Monthly
Emancipator
Frederick Douglass' Paper
Freedom's Journal
Genius of Universal Emancipation
Herald of Freedom
Independent
Liberator
National Anti-Slavery Standard
National Era
National Intelligencer
New York Times
New York Tribune
North Star
Pennsylvania Freeman
Philadelphia Inquirer
Philanthropist
Ram's Horn
Saturday Visiter

BOOKS

Bacon, Jacqueline. *Freedom's Journal: The First African-American Newspaper.* Lanham, Md.: Lexington Books, 2007.

Baldasty, Gerald J. *The Commercialization of News in the Nineteenth Century.* Madison: University of Wisconsin Press, 1992.

Barnes, Gilbert Hobbs. *The Antislavery Impulse, 1830–1844.* New York: Harcourt, Brace and World, 1964.

Blight, David W., ed. *Passages to Freedom: The Underground Railroad in History and Memory.* Washington, D.C.: Smithsonian Books, 2004.

Bradley, Patricia. *Women and the Press: The Struggle for Equality.* Evanston, Ill.: Northwestern University Press, 2005.

Campbell, Stanley W. *The Slave Catchers: Enforcement of the Fugitive Slave Law, 1850–1860.* Chapel Hill: University of North Carolina Press, 1968.

Cooper, William J. *The South and the Politics of Slavery, 1828–1856.* Baton Rouge: Louisiana State University Press, 1978.

Cornish, Dudley Taylor. *The Sable Arm: Negro Troops in the Union Army, 1861–1865.* New York: W. W. Norton, 1966.

Curtis, Michael Kent. *Free Speech: "The People's Darling Privilege."* Durham, N.C.: Duke University Press, 2000.

Davis, David Brion. *The Slave Power Conspiracy and the Paranoid Style.* Baton Rouge: Louisiana State University Press, 1969.

Davis, Hugh. *Joshua Leavitt, Evangelical Abolitionist.* Baton Rouge: Louisiana State University Press, 1990.

Dicken-Garcia, Hazel. *Journalistic Standards in Nineteenth-Century America.* Madison: University of Wisconsin Press, 1989.

Dillon, Merton L. *Benjamin Lundy and the Struggle for Negro Freedom.* Urbana: University of Illinois Press, 1966.

———. *Elijah P. Lovejoy, Abolitionist Editor.* Urbana: University of Illinois Press, 1964.

———. *Slavery Attacked: Southern Slaves and Their Allies.* Baton Rouge: Louisiana State University Press, 1990.

Donald, David. *Lincoln.* New York: Simon and Schuster, 1995.

Douglass, Frederick. *My Bondage and My Freedom.* New York: Penguin, 2003.

Drake, Thomas E. *Quakers and Slavery in America*. Gloucester, Mass.: Peter Smith, 1965.

Dumond, Dwight Lowell. *Antislavery Origins of the Civil War in the United States*. Ann Arbor: University of Michigan Press, 1959.

Durden, Robert F. *The Gray and the Black: The Confederate Debate on Emancipation*. Baton Rouge: Louisiana State University Press, 1972.

Eaton, Clement. *Freedom of Thought in the Old South*. Durham, N.C.: Duke University Press, 1940.

Fehrenbacher, Don E. *The Slaveholding Republic: An Account of the United States Government's Relations to Slavery*. New York: Oxford University Press, 2001.

Feldberg, Michael. *The Turbulent Era: Riot and Disorder in Jacksonian America*. New York: Oxford University Press, 1980.

Filler, Louis. *The Crusade Against Slavery, 1830–1860*. New York: Harper and Row, 1960.

Fladeland, Betty. *James Gillespie Birney: Slaveholder to Abolitionist*. Ithaca, N.Y.: Cornell University Press, 1955.

Foner, Eric. *Free Soil, Free Labor, Free Men: The Ideology of the Republican Party Before the Civil War*. New York: Oxford University Press, 1970.

———. *A Short History of Reconstruction, 1863–1877*. New York: Harper and Row, 1990.

Foner, Philip, ed. *The Life and Writings of Frederick Douglass*. 4 vols. New York: International Publishers, 1950.

Franklin, John Hope. *From Slavery to Freedom: A History of American Negroes*. New York: Alfred A. Knopf, 1947.

Gara, Larry. *The Liberty Line: The Legend of the Underground Railroad*. Lexington: University of Kentucky Press, 1961.

Gatewood, Willard B., Jr. *Free Man of Color: The Autobiography of Willis Augustus Hodges*. Knoxville: University of Tennessee Press, 1982.

Gienapp, William E. *The Origins of the Republican Party, 1852–1856*. New York: Oxford University Press, 1987.

———, ed. *This Fiery Trial: The Speeches and Writings of Abraham Lincoln*. New York: Oxford University Press, 2002.

Gossett, Thomas F. *"Uncle Tom's Cabin" and American Literature*. Dallas: Southern Methodist University Press, 1985.

Grimstead, David C. *American Mobbing, 1828–1861: Toward Civil War*. New York: Oxford University Press, 1998.

Guelzo, Allen C. *Lincoln's Emancipation Proclamation: The End of Slavery in America*. New York: Simon and Schuster, 2004.

Harper, Robert S. *Lincoln and the Press*. New York: McGraw-Hill, 1951.

Harrold, Stanley. *Gamaliel Bailey and Antislavery Union*. Kent, Ohio: Kent State University Press, 1986.

Hoffert, Sylvia D. *Jane Grey Swisshelm: An Unconventional Life, 1815–1884*. Chapel Hill: University of North Carolina Press, 2004.

Holt, Michael F. *The Political Crisis of the 1850s*. New York: W. W. Norton, 1978.

Hudson, Frederick. *Journalism in the United States, from 1690 to 1872*. New York: Harper and Brothers, 1873.

Huntzicker, William E. *The Popular Press, 1833–1865*. Westport, Conn.: Greenwood, 1999.

Hutton, Frankie. *The Early Black Press in America, 1827 to 1860*. Westport, Conn.: Greenwood, 1993.

Hutton, Frankie, and Barbara Reed, eds. *Outsiders in 19th-Century Press History: Multicultural Perspectives*. Bowling Green, Ohio: Bowling Green University Press, 1995.

Jeffrey, Julie Roy. *The Great Silent Army of Abolitionism: Ordinary Women in the Antislavery Movement*. Chapel Hill: University of North Carolina Press, 1998.

Karcher, Carolyn L. *The First Woman in the Republic: A Cultural Biography of Lydia Maria Child*. Durham, N.C.: Duke University Press, 1994.

Kessler, Lauren. *The Dissident Press: Alternative Journalism in American History*. Beverly Hills, Calif.: Sage, 1984.

Kirkham, Bruce E. *The Building of Uncle Tom's Cabin*. Knoxville: University of Tennessee Press, 1977.

Kirkland, Edward Chase. *The Peacemakers of 1864*. New York: Macmillan, 1927.

Kraditor, Aileen S. *Means and Ends in American Abolitionism: Garrison and His Critics on Strategy and Tactics, 1834–1850*. New York: Pantheon Books, 1967.

Litwack, Leon F. *Been in the Storm So Long: The Aftermath of Slavery.* Alfred A. Knopf: New York, 1979.

――――. *North of Slavery: The Negro in the Free States, 1790–1860.* Chicago: University of Chicago Press, 1961.

Lundy, Benjamin, and Thomas Earle, comps. *The Life, Travels, and Opinions of Benjamin Lundy.* New York: Negro Universities Press, 1969.

Malin, James C. *John Brown and the Legend of Fifty-Six.* Philadelphia: American Philosophical Society, 1942.

Mayer, Henry. *All on Fire: William Lloyd Garrison and the Abolition of Slavery.* New York: St. Martin's Press, 1998.

McFeely, William S. *Frederick Douglass.* New York: W. W. Norton, 1991.

McPherson, James M. *Battle Cry of Freedom: The Civil War Era.* New York: Oxford University Press, 1988.

――――. *The Negro's Civil War: How American Negroes Felt and Acted During the War for the Union.* New York: Pantheon Books, 1965.

――――. *Struggle for Equality: Abolitionists and the Negro in the Civil War and Reconstruction.* Princeton, N.J.: Princeton University Press, 1964.

Meer, Sarah. *Uncle Tom Mania: Slavery, Minstrelsy and Transatlantic Culture in the 1850s.* Athens: University of Georgia Press, 2005.

Merrill, Walter. *Against Wind and Tide: A Biography of William Lloyd Garrison.* Cambridge, Mass.: Harvard University Press, 1963.

Mott, Frank Luther. *A History of American Magazines, Volume II: 1850–1865.* Cambridge, Mass.: Harvard University Press, 1938.

Nerone, John. *The Culture of the Press in the Early Republic: Cincinnati, 1793–1848.* New York: Garland, 1989.

――――. *Violence Against the Press: Policing the Public Sphere in U.S. History.* New York: Oxford University Press, 1994.

Newman, Richard S. *The Transformation of American Abolitionism: Fighting Slavery in the Early Republic.* Chapel Hill: University of North Carolina Press, 2002.

Nye, Russel B. *Fettered Freedom: Civil Liberties and the Slavery Controversy, 1830–1860.* East Lansing: Michigan State University Press, 1963.

Oakes, James. *The Radical and the Republican: Frederick Douglass, Abraham Lincoln, and the Triumph of Antislavery Politics.* New York: W. W. Norton, 2007.

Oates, Stephen B. *To Purge This Land with Blood: A Biography of John Brown.* New York: Harper and Row, 1970.

Pease, Jane H., and William H. Pease. *Bound with Them in Chains: A Biographical History of the Antislavery Movement.* Westport, Conn.: Greenwood, 1972.

Penn, I. Garland. *The Afro-American Press and Its Editors.* New York: Arno, 1969.

Pollard, John A. *John Greenleaf Whittier, Friend of Man.* Boston: Houghton Mifflin, 1949.

Potter, David M. *The Impending Crisis, 1848–1861.* New York: Harper and Row, 1976.

Pride, Armistead S., and Clint C. Wilson II. *A History of the Black Press.* Washington, D.C.: Howard University Press, 1977.

Quarles, Benjamin. *Black Abolitionists.* New York: Oxford University Press, 1969.

———. *Frederick Douglass.* Washington, D.C.: Associated Publishers, 1948.

Randall, James G. *The Civil War and Reconstruction.* New York: Heath, 1937.

Ratner, Lorman. *Powder Keg: Northern Opposition to the Antislavery Movement, 1831–1840.* New York: Basic Books, 1968.

Ratner, Lorman A., and Dwight L. Teeter Jr. *Fanatics and Fire-Eaters: Newspapers and the Coming of the Civil War.* Urbana: University of Illinois Press, 2003.

Rawley, James A. *Race and Politics: "Bleeding Kansas" and the Coming of the Civil War.* Philadelphia: J. B. Lippincott, 1969.

Reynolds, Donald E. *Editors Make War: Southern Newspapers in the Secession Crisis.* Nashville, Tenn.: Vanderbilt University Press, 1966.

Richards, Leonard. *"Gentlemen of Property and Standing": Anti-Abolition Mobs in Jacksonian America.* New York: Oxford University Press, 1970.

Risley, Ford. *The Civil War: Primary Documents on Events from 1860 to 1865.* Westport, Conn.: Greenwood, 2004.

Ruchames, Louis, ed. *The Abolitionists: A Collection of Their Writings.* New York: Capricorn Books, 1963.

Sewell, Richard H. *Ballots for Freedom: Antislavery Politics in the United States, 1837–1860.* New York: Oxford University Press, 1976.

Sloan, Wm. David, ed. *Media and Religion in American History.* Northport, Ala.: Vision, 2000.

Stampp, Kenneth M. *The Peculiar Institution: Slavery in the Antebellum South.* New York: Alfred A. Knopf, 1956.

Starr, Louis M. *Bohemian Brigade: Civil War Newsmen in Action.* New York: Knopf, 1954.

Stewart, James Brewer. *Holy Warriors: The Abolitionists and American Slavery.* New York: Hill and Wang, 1976.

Streitmatter, Rodger. *Raising Her Voice: African-American Women Journalists Who Changed History.* Lexington: University Press of Kentucky, 1994.

Swisshelm, Jane Grey. *Half a Century.* Chicago: Jansen, McClurg, 1880.

Thomas, John L. *The Liberator, William Lloyd Garrison: A Biography.* Boston: Little, Brown, 1963.

Tripp, Bernell. *Origins of the Black Press: New York, 1827–1847.* Northport, Ala.: Vision, 1992.

Van Deusen, Glyndon G. *Horace Greeley, Nineteenth-Century Crusader.* New York: Hill and Wang, 1953.

Walters, Ronald G. *American Reformers, 1815–1860.* New York: Hill and Wang, 1978.

———. *The Antislavery Appeal: American Abolitionism After 1830.* Baltimore: Johns Hopkins University Press, 1976.

Washburn, Patrick S. *The African American Newspaper: Voice of Freedom.* Evanston, Ill.: Northwestern University Press, 2006.

Williams, T. Harry. *Lincoln and the Radicals.* Madison: University of Wisconsin Press, 1960.

Woodward, C. Vann. *The Burden of Southern History.* Baton Rouge: Louisiana Sate University Press, 1960.

Wyatt-Brown, Bertram. *Lewis Tappan and the Evangelical War Against Slavery.* Cleveland: Press of Case Western Reserve University, 1969.

————. *Yankee Saints and Southern Sinners*. Baton Rouge: Louisiana State University Press, 1985.

ARTICLES

Bryan, Carter R. "Negro Journalism in America Before Emancipation." *Journalism Monographs* 12 (September 1969): 1–33.

Davis, David Brion. "The Emergence of Immediatism in British and American Antislavery Thought." *Mississippi Valley Historical Review* 49 (September 1962): 209–30.

Dillon, Merton L. "The Failure of American Abolitionists." *Journal of Southern History* 25 (March 1959): 159–77.

Eaton, Clement. "The Freedom of the Press in the Upper South." *Mississippi Valley Historical Review* 18 (March 1932): 479–99.

Endres, Kathleen L. "Jane Grey Swisshelm: 19th Century Journalist and Feminist." *Journalism History* 2 (Winter 1975): 128–32.

Filler, Louis. "Liberalism, Anti-Slavery, and the Founders of the *Independent*." *New England Quarterly* 27 (September 1954): 291–306.

Franklin, Cathy Rogers. "James Gillespie Birney, the Revival Spirit, and *The Philanthropist*." *American Journalism* 17 (Spring 2000): 31–51.

Gara, Larry. "Slavery and the Slave Power: A Crucial Distinction." *Civil War History* 17 (March 1969): 5–18.

Gross, Bella. "*Freedom's Journal* and the *Rights of All*." *Journal of Negro History* 17 (July 1932): 241–86.

Kielbowicz, Richard B. "The Law and Mob Law in Attacks on Antislavery Newspapers, 1833–1860." *Law and History Review* 24 (Fall 2006): 559–600.

Martin, Asa E. "Pioneer Anti-Slavery Press." *Mississippi Valley Historical Review* 2 (1925): 509–28.

Nord, David Paul. "The Evangelical Origins of Mass Media in America, 1815–1835." *Journalism Monographs* 88 (May 1984): 1–30.

Nordin, Kenneth. "In Search of Black Unity: An Interpretation of the Content and Function of *Freedom's Journal*." *Journalism History* 4 (Winter 1977): 123–38.

Nye, Russell B. "Freedom of the Press and the Antislavery Contro-versy." *Journalism Quarterly* 22 (March 1945): 1–11.

Pease, Jane H., and William H. Pease. "Confrontation and Aboli-tion in the 1850s." *Journal of American History* 63 (March 1972): 923–37.

Risley, Ford. "The Savannah Morning News as a Penny Paper: Inde-pendent, but Hardly Neutral." *American Journalism* 16 (Fall 1999): 19-36.

Simms, Henry. "A Critical Analysis of Abolition Literature." *Journal of Southern History* 6 (August 1940): 368–82.

Stampp, Kenneth M. "The Fate of the Southern Antislavery Move-ment." *Journal of Negro History* 12 (January 1943): 10–22.

Stewart, James B. "The Aims and Impact of Garrisonian Abolitionism, 1840–1860." *Civil War History* 15 (September 1969): 197–209.

Wyatt-Brown, Bertram. "The Abolitionists' Postal Campaign of 1835." *Journal of Negro History* 50 (October 1965): 227–38.

———. "William Lloyd Garrison and Antislavery Union: A Reap-praisal." *Civil War History* 13 (March 1967): 5–24.

INDEX

Ford Risley is the head of the journalism department at the College of Communications at Penn State University, where he has taught since 1995. He is the author of *The Civil War: Primary Documents on Events from 1860 to 1865*. He lives in State College, Pennsylvania.